Finding My Way in a Strange Land
John E. Brooks, BEM, an Anguillan in Britain

by

John E. Brooks, BEM with
Whitman T. Browne, Ph.D.

To JOHN & JEAN

Friends are for ever and not only the odd
occasion when we met

E Bro

31/8/12

DORRANCE PUBLISHING CO., INC.
PITTSBURGH, PENNSYLVANIA 15222

Dorrance Publishing Co., Inc.
701 Smithfield Street
Pittsburgh, PA 15222
Visit our website at www.dorrancebookstore.com

ISBN: 978-1-4349-1616-7
eISBN: 978-1-4349-1565-8

Finding My Way in a Strange Land: The Story of John E. Brooks, BEM, An Anguillan in Britain

John E. Brooks, BEM
with
Whitman T. Browne, Ph.D.

Contents

JOHN E. BROOKS, B. E. M., JP.

Critical Events and Highlights of My Life

1955:   1st October arrived in UK from Anguilla. I intended to stay for five years.

1958:   Called to do two years of compulsory British National Service. I did twenty-six years.

1959:   Experienced a serious motorcycle accident. I was lucky to have survived.

1960:   Married to Audrey Arrindell, a nursing student from St. Kitts, on June 25, 1960. We have three children and two grandchildren.

1962:   First posting outside Britain, to Celle, Germany.

1965:   Shifted foreign posting from Germany to Singapore.

1968:   First trip back to Anguilla after leaving in 1955.

1968:   New posting at Bielefeld Germany.

1968:   Transferred from Germany to Belgium for six months, then back to Munster, Germany in six months.

1971:   Stationed in Britain again at Oxfordshire and Surrey.

1974:   First endurance walk, a fundraiser for the National Society for Prevention of Cruelty to Children (NSPCC).

1974:   Became the British, European and Commonwealth endurance walking record holder. From May 24 to 29, walked 290 miles nonstop. From June 29 to July 4, walked 291.75 miles nonstop.

1975:   Was listed in the *Guinness Book of Records* as a champion of endurance walking.

1975:   Visited the War Office to make a special cassette recording for the British forces in Germany.

1976:   Nominated and awarded the British Empire Medal (BEM), as special recognition by Her Majesty Queen Elizabeth II, during one of the ceremonies for her Birthday Honors List

1976: Invited to spend a day visiting both the House of Commons and the Houses of Parliament.

1976: New foreign assignment to Brunei. Considered the most unpleasant of my military career.

1976: Shifted from Brunei to Hong Kong. While in Hong Kong, I visited mainland China and Bangkok.

1979: Stationed back in Britain, in the Warwickshire area. Completed my last five years of military service there.

1982: Involved in setting up a special military display for Her Majesty Queen II. There I was introduced to Queen Elizabeth II in person.

1984: March 24 was the end of my military service.

1984: Started out as a self-employed businessman. I opened a nursing home.

1985: Ventured into politics.

1986: Nominated and became a magistrate.

1998: Built a house in Anguilla.

2000: Nominated as a local Town Councillor.

2003: Retired from business.

2005: Nominated to serve as Mayor of Banbury (2005-2006).

Special Awards:

2004: From the government of Anguilla, for contributions to the Social Development of Anguillans and the Advancement of All Mankind.

2009: Award from Anguilla Progressive Association: For achievements in the UK and in Anguilla.

MEDIA COVERAGE:

Local and national press, international press, including television, for example, in Hong Kong, Canada, Anguilla, and elsewhere. Also, I took part in movie screening.

Countries Visited:

Germany, Belgium, France, Holland, Norway, Denmark, Singapore, Malaysia, Brunei, Hong Kong, Malta, China, Canada, USA, Bangkok, Turkey, and numerous Caribbean Islands.

Chapter One

Reflections on My Life in Anguilla

I was born on the tiny Caribbean island of Anguilla in 1935. But I am no longer there, I live in Britain. Every now and then, memories of those early experiences I shared on that island come flooding back into my mind. Very often, I see images of Hope Cottage, the very picturesque house where I grew up, as well as the many beaches around the island, where my friends, sisters, brothers, and I loved to romp and swim. The boys went to an all-boys primary school, while the girls went to an all-girls school. Our single sex schools were a legacy from the time when the British Government neglected its responsibility to educate and empower the people in its colonies. The island's early education system was therefore designed and dominated by the Anglican and Methodist churches up until 1915. A decision was made by the church run schools that it would lead to sexual immorality if boys and girls in the colonies were educated in the same classes and schools, even at the elementary level. For a secondary education, one had to go off-island, preferably to St. Kitts, the largest island and controlling partner in the three islands British colony—St. Kitts, Nevis, and Anguilla. Few Anguillans could afford that cost or understood the real value of such an investment then. Actually, access to public secondary education did not become available on Anguilla until about 1953. It has a much long history on St. Kitts.

Regular churchgoing started for me as a young boy when I attended the Methodist Church every Sunday, with my parents and siblings. . Today, I still make the time and attend the Methodist Church as frequently as I can, whether I am at home or travelling. This practice which I started years ago on Anguilla, still brings a certain solace and healing to my life.

My parents were Inez Winifred Brooks and Ernest Adalbert Brooks. My brothers and sisters consisted of seven siblings: five girls and two boys, besides myself, in my family. I can still hear the loud sounds of my sisters and brothers as we competed with one another, as we argued among ourselves, and as we played together in our house. Back then, the average Caribbean family was larger, four, six, and eight children were common. During that time, making a success of life for families in Anguilla and other Caribbean islands was often challenging and uncertain. By the 1950s the islands had been depleted of their economic resources by the colonizers and limited attention had been paid to educating the mass of poor children on the islands. Accordingly, emigration from the island held a powerful attraction to young and older males, and in time for some females too.

At all levels of that society, social distance mattered. Parents were treated with respect. Children acted with a certain reverence to all older persons. Preachers and teachers were virtually revered. At the same time, the poorer and lower class society paid homage and treated those who were wealthier with certain natural and traditional respect taught by the colonizing British. There was also special umbrage to skin color, with those of lighter shades having a sense of superiority. Generally, however, people respected one another in a society where the extended family played an important role in the transmission of the island's cultural ideals:, values, folklore, thinking about the world, and how the future was to be perceived. Within that special family unit, usually with grandparents, parents, and at times aunts, uncles, cousins, and close knit neighbors, there was often a classic realization of the idea, "a village raising the children."

Our father did many things to make a living and support his family. There were times when this took him to other islands beyond Anguilla, to St. Martin, to Antigua, to St. Kitts, and to elsewhere in the Caribbean. He also worked for the Department of Agriculture, did some fishing, and farmed to produce his own crops. Meanwhile, my mother worked at home and helped to provide for our large family. Back then, there was no argument about whether mothers should stay at home and look after the children. Few Caribbean men wanted their wives to work outside the home, then. However, there were those who could not afford to do differently, and who allowed their wives to be employed by others. Women had to work outside the home in agricultural production, as maids, or elsewhere, because the family was large and the father's earnings were often meager, not enough to maintain the home.

Our mother enjoyed baking bread, so she baked extra bread for sale. At times, she also made certain that our less fortunate neighbours, though unable to buy the bread, did not go hungry. Such persons were provided free bread on a regular basis. I continue to remember my mother reaching out to help many very poor and indigent persons in our community. Few of the Afro-Caribbean people at the time lived better than comfortable. Maybe it was those pictures of my mother reaching out to help others less fortunate than we were that have influenced my own interest in charities through the years. Today, I still get good feelings when I visit Anguilla, and persons on the island remind me about the generosity of my parents, the things they did to share with and help others who were less fortunate in the community.

I also recall that there were pleasant experiences with my uncles, aunts, and cousins. They visited us from time to time, and at other times my family would stop by to see them, too. Back then, the Caribbean islands were much further from one another because of travel limitations. . However, it was not always a whole era that passed before there was some form of family reunions. Those who went abroad returned every now and then. Family was precious despite sibling squabbles. The emotional and other support from family relationships also mattered greatly, particularly in bad times. And there were frequent bad times in the Caribbean islands. At some point each one has suffered from droughts, hurricanes, and the inevitable loss of loved ones to death. Such experiences, coupled with the economic and financial frugality of the British in dealing with its colonies, often left the islanders dependent and struggling with a situation of persistent poverty.

On a small island such as Anguilla, even the children knew almost everyone else in their communities. People in such societies, often discovered, again and again, that they needed one another. Their survival depended on maintaining some level of interdependence. This situation increasingly became a reality since by the end of the 1800s, the colonies in the Caribbean were becoming an increased financial burden to Britain, Holland, France, and Denmark... At the same time, the Afro-Caribbean people on the islands were angry with their condition of neglect, poverty, and second class citizenship, which the European Governments fostered in their Caribbean colonies. For example, unlike the USA, Britain was miserly with its financial support to its colonies. However, at an earlier time, when sugar was profitable in the islands, Britain exploited aggressively, the resources from the same Caribbean islands, to enhance its own economic, social, and military development. Later on, because of its better and more successful sugar production, St. Kitts, not Britain, was made responsible for managing and financing itself, along with Anguilla and Nevis. The British Government gave very little economic contribution to the colony. By the 1950s, when I contemplated emigrating from Anguilla, the contribution of the British Government to the financial upkeep of Anguilla, St. Kitts, and Nevis was far less than what the United States of America was providing for both of its two Caribbean colonies, the Virgin Islands and Puerto Rico, not far away.

At that time, Anguilla had a population of a little over 6,000 people. It was a hardy, sea-faring, and restless population which struggled to make life on the island. The soil was not as friendly to agriculture as on Nevis or even more so on St. Kitts. Anguilla is of coral formation, has no high land elevation that can be called a mountain, and gets limited rainfall. The island is also burdened with very shallow soil. Fishing and sailing have always been popular attractions to Anguillans. However, a large salt pond in the Sandy Ground area was very productive at one time and supplied salt, which was traded to some of the surrounding islands. Notwithstanding, life on the island was often monotonous. Many young Anguillan men felt corralled in on an island without too much promise for their future. They often chose to move away from the drudgery of life on the island to follow dreams of a better, more productive life. Like many other West Indian migrants, Anguillans left their island not so much in search of fame or because of anger derived from a criticism of colonialism. They were reaching beyond their island in search of fortune, adventure, and physical survival. Many migrated to St. Martin nearby, to St. Kitts, some seventy miles across the Caribbean Sea, and often to places much further away, including the British and US Virgin Islands, Curacao, the USA, and later to Britain. Whatever the costs, Anguillan men have been leaving their island and chasing dreams, from as far back as the late 1800s. For them those dreams were not illusions. The grass was much greener beyond Anguilla. Growth experiences for the men and women on the island were limited, too competitive and often never came. It was too limiting for them, for their children, and for the future.

Educating the working class who labored on the plantations in the islands was not of great interest to the British Government or the elite plantation owners. Although Anguilla was not a very successful plantation economy, the matter of focusing on and developing public education in the island was not an easy matter for the ruling elite to agree on. Thus the issue of educating working-class children on the islands remained unresolved and a debated matter for many years. As noted, it was not until the early 1900s that educating the masses in its colonies was accepted as a responsibility for the colonizing British Government.

Prior to that time, attempts at educating the mass of children on the island was a task relegated to the Methodist, the Anglican, and the Roman Catholic churches on the islands. It was a philanthropic endeavour for their parishioners. There is also the argument that the churches used religion then as a social control strategy. During those years, the mass of children on the islands were limited to a primary education, which ended at grade seven, or before. It was basic education with focus on reading, writing, and arithmetic. Some of the materials taught in the islands' schools were prepared specially for schools in the colonies. Often it carefully replicated the education that was given in the British school system. In one of his popular calypsos, *Dan is the Man in the Van*, the Mighty Sparrow, one of the Caribbean's leading calypsonians, poked fun at the colonial education system in the Caribbean during the 1950s and 1960s. It did not take Caribbean history, culture or the development of the people, into account.

During that time, very few students from the working class had real dreams of entering secondary schools, or attending university for an education. Higher education was a privileged experience for the elite. Consequently, for many years on the islands, university education was for a select group in the Caribbean. It was uncommon for boys and girls to be educated together in the same church-run schools. Accordingly, girls and boys went to separate schools. For a number of years, a viable public secondary education was available only on St. Kitts at one time, and it was for a chosen few. The colonial society was also very selective about which few that was. I attended the Valley Boys School for my primary education. Vehicles were rare on the island then, so everyone walked to school. For me, the distance walked was three quarters of a mile each way, to and from school. I also walked home and back to school during lunchtime. We got about one hour for lunch. A public secondary school, the Anguilla Secondary School, was eventually set up on the island during the early 1950s. It limited the travel to other islands for secondary education, by Anguillans. The building of that school on Anguilla also started a long process of democratizing higher education on the island, since it gave working-class children hope for participation and eventual change in the education programme.

My brothers and sisters were more committed to an academic education and consistently showed themselves to be better students than I was. It was also possible that my mother talked to them about the value of education more than she did to me, since she noticed that I was otherwise inclined. To me at that time, school seemed to be boring, and I did not see its connection with real life. I recall being happier assisting my parents with assignments at home and working in the land, than being at school. I had more fun doing things with my hands. Accordingly, I was always ready to assist my father on the farm, where he cultivated sea-island cotton, at the area called The Valley Bottom. When I left school in the afternoons, I spent a great deal of my time working there with him. At times, too, I helped my mother with her baking in a brick oven. It was made from lime, sand, brick, and had to be heated to the operational temperature by stocking it with firewood. The wood was then set alight and allowed to burn until it became ash. Once I became older, I was shown how to travel to a location about one and a half miles from home, where I collected the firewood we needed for baking.

Seemingly, my lack of interest in formal schooling was noticed by my parents, but I do not recall discussing the matter with them. While we hardly spoke about school, my mother did suggest early that I become an apprentice to one of the tradesmen in the area. She was concerned that I made something of myself, and probably had no intention that I become an embarrassment to the Brooks family. Accordingly, I was not deprived of opportunities for success. In varied areas of my life, I was offered opportunities for all-round personal development. For example, my parents insisted that I got tutoring in music, French, and at one time I also considered a correspondence course in diesel engines and mechanics.

My apprenticeship experience in carpentry was started before I finished school. The trade offerings were boat-building, tailoring, shoe repair, and carpentry. Tailoring and shoe repair were too sedentary for my liking. I therefore opted to learn carpentry and boat-building. Besides keeping me actively engaged, these were trades I saw as useful in that the skills I learned would enable me to do creative things such as making furniture and boats, things which were usually in demand on the island. On leaving school, I was sent to work with my brothers-in-law, Herman and Sylvanus Lloyd, as an apprentice. The experience was exciting and useful for me. Not long into the apprenticeship, I became good enough to accept jobs from persons in the community and worked independently. I also got jobs to change wooden blinds to glass sashes. At that time, I participated in installing some of the first glass windows to be made on the island...

In retrospect, I see my schooling back then as countering the popular argument that one's early education prepares him or her for life. Not long after, I travelled beyond the island and encountered a totally different cultural experience from that I knew where I grew up. Probably, my capacity to adapt and learn from new experiences was more helpful to me than the formal education I received on the island. While it did contribute to my overall growth, I am not certain how much that education prepared me for the life I came to live beyond Anguilla. Notwithstanding, I have forever been haunted by the fact that I was not as academically talented and as successful as my brothers and sisters, during my school days in Anguilla.

During the period when I grew up, children went to church with their parents on a regular basis. Church was a Sunday routine and never questioned by them. My parents were Methodists, so I accompanied them to that church. There was little more that was done by young people on Sundays. Often we would attend church then visit the beaches. I went to church three times every Sunday. There was also an added incentive for regular attendance. A special prize was awarded to those who had perfect Sunday-school attendance for a year. Since my brothers and sisters did not think that I tried hard enough to be academic and scholarly, at times, they snubbed and criticised me. However, while I was not a fluent reader, when I received a role in a Sunday school play, I was able to get on the stage and performed with comfort and confidence. I could even recite my lines, without looking at the paper.

Despite that measure of success at Sunday school, I remember that my oldest sister, Ruby, took pleasure in humiliating me. There were times when she had me stand on stage and repeat, "I am a duncy head." I still recall and cringe at that humbling experience because of the way it made me feel. In the end, however, my sister's criticism and insensitivity did not prevent me from achieving the fundamentals of a primary education as I attended school and church on Anguilla. Those experiences might have helped my all-round preparation for future success. Today, I look back at such situations without animosity, and at times even smile about some things I once saw as storms in my life. Admittedly, I was exposed to the same opportunities as my brothers and sisters to become academically successful. However, I chose to set my own path in life. It was different from the one they took. Further, there were some things which I opted to do the hard way. For me then, there was no other way than my way.

All eight of us, the Brooks children, knew how to share and help one another. At that time in the West Indies, large families were common and were usually held together by a strong mother or father, along with their extended family connections. In my family, even as we grew up and went our separate ways we remained in close contact. However, there were favorites within our family relations. As I look back through time, I still think my mother had a special place in her heart for me. Only one of us stayed at home in Anguilla and did not venture abroad. That was Sister Audrey. She stayed at home and became contact person to us abroad, and care-giver to our parents there, as they became older. The others of us helped financially as was necessary. That was a common practice in the Caribbean back then. The area became caught up in migration, ongoing political and social change, but there was no proper planning or accommodation for the aged back then. Usually one child remained at home with the parents and filled in for the other children who paid occasional visits, or contributed money towards their parents' upkeep. My favourite sister was Maude, the second sister. She got married at a young age and had a large family. But I could always count on her for help if I ever needed anything from her. I still hold fond memories of Maude.

West Indian people have a long history of migration throughout the Caribbean area and to elsewhere in the world. Because of its limited capacity for successful agricultural production, Anguilla, like Nevis, has a long history of high unemployment and a migrating, shifting population, willing to move through the Caribbean area, or elsewhere, in search of employment and adventure. After the Second World War, Britain needed laborers as it made an unprecedented move towards its re-development. It invited workers from the varied countries and islands it still controlled as colonies, to come, live, and work in Britain. The offer was readily accepted in the West Indies. Thousands of people from the colonies that Britain exploited for hundreds of years made the decision to leave the West Indies and live in Britain. It was two-way culture shock, as thousands of its colonised subjects opted to live and work in Britain. Others went there from Africa and Asia. Just as it did during the 1700s and 1800s, during the 1900s, Britain turned again to its Caribbean colonies to help rebuild itself. Citizens from those colonies had also fought for Britain in WW I and WW II. After 1945, the nation needed cheap labour again to rebuild itself and to transform its economy. Fortunately, during the 1900s, the labour used to develop Britain was more voluntary and by choice, rather than being coerced.

Like other persons from the many British West Indian colonies, Anguillans too, responded to the call and moved to Britain in search of a better life. In time, I too, had to face the matter and decide whether I wanted to leave Anguilla to live in England. My uncle, Bertram Daniel, who served as a policeman in Antigua, was set against the idea of me migrating to England. He wanted to see me join the Leeward Islands Police Force and work in Antigua where he held a position as a police officer. I met Uncle Bertram or Buttie for the first time in 1953, the year of Queen Elizabeth II's coronation. He visited Anguilla shortly after the coronation to see his mother and my grandmother, Maude Daniel. I still remember my special gifts from Uncle Buttie. They were a coronation cup and a policeman's helmet. My uncle obviously thought he could get me into the Leeward Islands Police Force without much difficulty. Our relationship with Uncle Bertram was to become closer because, as we travelled around later, on many occasions we spent time in Antigua when we could not get to Anguilla until the next day. Over time, his address at 91 Bishop Gate Street, St. John's, Antigua became well known and could be rattled off readily by all of us.

For most West Indians, the journey to England, during the 1940s, 1950s and 1960s, was long, intimidating, and held the prospect of strange unusual weather conditions. The people and culture were also quite different from those known in the Caribbean. However, Caribbean people were facing desperate economic and untenable social conditions at home during the 1950s; despite their remarkable capacity to innovate and survive under unusual circumstances. Meanwhile, they learned and grew as they travelled around. Many of us took great joy in sharing their new experiences with friends and family on their return home. Caribbean migrations helped to make important and profound transformations in the islands. By 1955, a number of Anguillans were already settled in England. Those who were there soon began to invite friends and family to share the new experiences away from home. At the same time, thousands of young West Indians, men in particular, were becoming increasingly disillusioned with the agricultural monopoly on their islands. There were also political and social concerns about high unemployment, the persistent poverty on many islands, and a growing return to dictatorship by political elites. Thousands of West Indians became anxious, as they waited for calls to live and work in other places around the world. The USA, Canada, and after the 1940s, Britain too, became the prime areas for Caribbean migrations.

I was turning twenty when my call from England came in January of 1955. Claude Brooks, a friend of my family, had moved from Anguilla to England at an earlier time. He wrote to my parents and suggested that they send me to live and work in England. My immediate response to the suggestion was, "Yes, I am ready to go." In the family, I always felt like the underdog because I performed so poorly in school. I was also convinced that the others looked down on me. Maybe, by moving away, I could get a new start and re-make my life different from what my family anticipated it would be.

Psychologically, I felt I could only find my way and make it in the world some place away from home and my siblings. I could not compete with them academically, and in Anguilla, that mattered!. The offer of a trip to England seemed to be the great get-away I was hoping for. I responded to my parents positively. The offer for travel to Britain was accepted, and immediately, they began to make arrangements for my travel to England. However, when my mom enquired about how much money I had to pay for the trip, I became very embarrassed. Although I worked regularly, I had not saved any money. Since they were very resourceful, however, my parents soon secured the money for the trip. I also started to wonder whether they wanted me to make the trip because they, too, thought I could make a better me there.

The planning for my travel to England continued and time passed. Uncle Bertram remained set against it, but my parents defied him. They were not interested in having me work as a policeman in Antigua. Soon, my suitcase was packed, set aside, secured, and ready for a quick move. It came towards the middle of September in 1955. I was at work when a message came from my mother stating that I would be leaving for England at 3:00 PM that day. Since my suitcase was ready and waiting, all I had to do was to change my clothes and be on my journey—a journey that would change my life profoundly.

Back in 1955, there were only two trucks on the island. I got one of them to transport me and my suitcase to the wharf at Forrest Bay. There I boarded the inter-island boat, *The Linda,* for St. Kitts. That was the first leg of my journey to Britain. When I got to St. Kitts, I would transfer to a steam-ship that had collected passengers from other islands, and was on its way to England. My eldest sister, Ruby, lived on St. Kitts and promised to meet me at the wharf in Basseterre, the capital, when the boat arrived from Anguilla. However, that was not to be. The wind did not favour smooth sailing for the boat. Accordingly, the captain decided to enter and dock at the first port he encountered on St. Kitts. We landed at Sandy Point instead of Basseterre. This was ten miles from where my sister had promised to meet me. I had to make other arrangements to meet her at Basseterre.

Ruby and I spent some days together before the ship for England came. Those few days with Ruby on St. Kitts were very precious to both of us. Neither of us knew when we would see each other again. During that time, with less advanced technology and slower transportation, England seemed so far away from the West Indies. Many persons were leaving to go there, but few of them were seen returning. Ruby and I went to church the Sunday and we realized that many other persons in the congregation were also about to leave the Caribbean for Britain. The preacher paid attention to that fact and gave us a parting challenge. He reminded us to remember our family and friends back on the islands. Then, he suggested to us, in his sermon, that "News from a far land is like water to a thirsty soul." It has been some fifty-six years, but I have not forgotten those words. I still find deep meaning in them. They helped to fashion my desire to stay in touch with the Caribbean.

Eventually, the time came for me to say goodbye to Sister Ruby and to the West Indies. So, I joined the many other passengers aboard the ship *S. S. Uriga.* Then, we were off to an eleven-day voyage to England. While I was curious and expectant about the idea of travelling to Britain, throughout the journey I struggled with an uneasy feeling. There I was, a young man who had grown up on Anguilla, and had spent all of my twenty years there. Suddenly, there I was, leaving the warm Caribbean behind to face an English winter for the first time. Admittedly, I was still quite naïve, and had no firm idea about the culture shock experience about to overwhelm my life. The one travelling was always advised by travel suggestions sent from persons already in England. However, for those making the journey for the first time, there would be a wide knowledge gap and much cultural adjustment, even to the point of culture shock. In 1955, my knowledge about England was limited. It was largely what I read in school books, what I heard from radio news, and what I gathered from discussions with other persons. I discovered later that very few of my expectations were reliable.

While I was preparing to leave Anguilla, I took time to share my important dreams with my parents. At the top of that list was my aim to work for about five years in England, gather enough money, then return to Anguilla and build my own house. That was how I dreamed, thought, and saw the world, fifty-six years ago. I knew little about life other than what I had seen and experienced in tiny, neglected Anguilla. Many years later, I did return and built the house in Anguilla. It took much longer than the five years I had originally planned. However, I still live in England. Through the past many years I have become accustomed to its unstable weather, learned the subtleties about its life and culture, and experienced the many peculiarities of British life. Today, it is with a smile that I reflect on that time, so very long ago, when I landed in England on a cold day in October, 1955. It still remains one of the coldest days I have experienced in my life. It was my baptism to life in Britain and winter weather. However, I was concerned, circumspect, but very committed to finding my way beyond Anguilla, my sunny Caribbean home, as I started my search for a new life in a strange cold land.

Chapter Two

From Anguilla to Britain

While I enjoyed playing in the warm, calm Caribbean Sea, running and frolicking on the white sandy beaches around Anguilla, sailing on the sea for eleven days was a different matter. As fate would have it, I was not a good passenger on the sea. And the size of the ship did not make much difference. The eleven-day sail to England proved to be a very humbling experience for me. During the entire journey, I vomited, had headache, and whenever I stood up, my whole body appeared to be twirling around. My ability to stand and balance myself was gone from me. For all that eleven days, I knew what it meant to be feeling "sick like a dog." The times when I was down were much more frequent than the times when I was up. I must have heard other passengers talk about the ship having had engine trouble, along the way, but I did not know the difference. For me, I was too dazed for that to matter. Instead, I kept being ill and was not very coherent at any point during the journey to remember much of what happened, other than my being ill. I recall that as we passed the Azores, the passengers were afforded the first sight of land after we left St. Kitts. We continued our voyage and arrived at Southampton about mid-day, October 1. However, when we got to Southampton, my personal journey was not over. One person meeting me was waiting at Waterloo. Then I had to travel on to Slough, in Buckinghamshire, some one hundred and ten miles beyond Southampton.

Notwithstanding, in light of the sea-sickness and my awful feeling, I was very happy to walk off the ship and onto the land in Southampton. I felt weak and wobbly from being a poor sailor, but I looked forward to regaining normalcy back on the land. For me, the journey from St. Kitts to Britain was an all-round horrible experience—one I would never like to repeat in my lifetime. Until then, I could not remember being so ill, or being ill for an eleven-day period, at any one time in my life.

Despite my weakened condition, I was very aware that I had entered a new country and would be subjected to new and different experiences. Being from a small island in the tropical Caribbean, I did not have a real picture of what to expect in cool, then cold, and by early afternoon, dark misty, Britain. My situation of naivety did not help my culture shock either. But, shortly after my first day in England, it came to my mind that I would have to stand on my own feet and learn fast, as I set out to find my way. One of my first of many initial problems, was the task of making my way to Waterloo Station with my suitcases and taking the train. At that time, all I knew about trains was what I read at school. Even if I had seen the picture of a train before, I had absolutely no knowledge about checking train schedules or how to board them. Back in Anguilla we walked, ran, or rode bicycles, and sometimes donkeys. At times I caught a truck, but never a train. There was no place for a train to run.

While I contemplated my train ride, I was still smarting from the stress of my eleven-day illness on the ship. That hang-over was coupled with the anxiety I felt, as I tried to follow the directions sent to me, so that I could make it to my final destination. At that time, I was also naïve to the fact that there was much further for me to go than I had ever travelled on land before. Actually, the first leg of my travel to Slough, in Buckinghamshire, was just the beginning. There were two other sections to that journey.

Since I was coming from tiny Anguilla, there was the additional drawback of my limited ability to grasp and appreciate the vast distance between places in Britain. Accordingly, it was decided that the best solution to my situation of ignorance and culture shock was to ask questions. Even then, I had some problems since the British accent and the dictions given were very strange to me. Admittedly, my accent and questions about dictions were strange to the British people, too.

From my first day in Britain, I got a positive impression about the respect and politeness displayed by the English people, then. They responded politely to my questions and gave me very good directions. Some even appeared to empathise with my situation of culture shock and "lost-ness." Accordingly, they too asked questions, as they helped me to find my way. I found the police to be approachable, friendly, and very helpful. Meanwhile, the size of the country and the distance to travel from one place to another, became factors which kept boggling my mind and challenging my imagination. Back in Anguilla almost every place I travelled was within a short walking distance. There was never the need for a map. Going ten miles from one place to another was considered very far. However, once I arrived in Britain, I discovered quickly that far meant a much greater distance than what I grew up knowing it to be. There was a vast difference between going ten miles on Anguilla, and travelling for hours in Britain, where one can travel over one hundred miles, or for many days, to a destination. In time, did get very good directions in response to my numerous enquiries. They helped me find my way to the Waterloo Station where someone was waiting to meet me. All throughout the experience, I thought about how strange, and how very different things were in Britain. They were far removed from what I knew back in Anguilla.

I soon learned that one of the many interesting phenomena about migrants is their ability to network and organise themselves for survival. In my case, I found that it was happening as early as just a few hours in my new land. At Waterloo Station I was met by a Methodist minister, Leonard Carty, now deceased, but then an Anguillan, studying in Reading. For me, that was a very welcoming encounter. Meeting someone whom I knew from home was a very reassuring experience at the time. It did not matter that we interacted for only a short period. After my time together with Mr. Carty, I was given the directions to Paddington Station. There I took another train and made my way to Cippingham in Slough, Buckinghamshire, my final destination.

During my early days in England, I was interested in learning more about the place, so I travelled around as often as I could. At times I went from Slough to London to meet friends. I also went to White City, where I was awed by the motor show. It was quite an educational experience for me to see all those fancy cars in the motor show. They were far more than existed on Anguilla. At first, I was naïve to the fact that I too could purchase an A-Z map and use it to help me get around. During such times, I often turned to the police when I needed help with finding my way. At first, the police were both kind and friendly to me. Unfortunately, that friendly posture that the British policemen displayed back in the 1950s is not always seen today. It has changed with the times and the circumstances, which have come to impact and change every aspect of British life through the years I have been living here.

Even after almost fifty-six years, my mind can still go back to the many strange but profound experiences I had on October 1, 1955, the first day of my arrival in England. First, I ended a long ocean journey that took a great deal from my spirit. Then I travelled for many miles by three different trains on my way to Buckinghamshire, my intended destination.

I had chosen to leave Anguilla, where I was warm and comfortable, to live in a land that I heard about, but did not know. However, from the time I landed at Southampton and as I made my way to Buckinghamshire, I became increasingly curious about, and intrigued with this strange land. It was so very different from mine., Yet it would soon become my new home. As quickly as was possible for me, I committed myself fully to start learning all I could about England. That time it was not second-hand from a book or hearsay. My new learning would be first-hand and personal, from my daily experiences.

For a young man at twenty years of age, making such a bold move from the small Caribbean to a much larger and strange Europe was a daunting challenge. I was not even certain whether I would see my family or my friends back in Anguilla again. But I was not alone. It was a risk that thousands of West Indians were willing to take. The West Indian Islands were warm, comfortable, charming, all with sandy beaches and some with beautiful rainforests. They are also surrounded by the soothing Caribbean Sea. However, the islands were also haunted by a lack of economic diversity, political uncertainty, persistent poverty and a need for greater educational opportunities for the masses, low levels of employment, drought, and hurricanes. At that time very little was being done by the islands' leadership to counter such problems. During the 1950s when I made my move from Anguilla to Britain, there was an almost unending movement of emigrants from my island, and from every other island in the Caribbean. Even in the US Virgin Islands and Puerto Rico, where the economy was much more vibrant because of the greater willingness by the US to invest financially in its colonies, there was a common desire almost everywhere to emigrate from the Caribbean area. Life was perceived to be better in America, in Britain, and elsewhere beyond the islands.

Making a move through, or away from the Caribbean, was always a daring adventure. There were times when thousands of the adventurers never saw the Caribbean area again. Some went back having lost their sanity during their new experience,, while others chose to deny their Caribbean experience and heritage. However, for generation after generation, that move to the larger, more vibrant and economically successful world beyond the Caribbean was a tried and true escape strategy for young West Indian men and women. For many of them, that trip helped them escape the persistent poverty fostered in their islands by Britain's colonial and economic policies. At times, there were conflict issues related to legality, health, and culture factors, but emigration was an adventure thousands of persons from the Caribbean were very willing to take. For example, while I was moving to England, other Anguillans were moving to St. Kitts, to St. Martin, to the US Virgin Islands, to Canada, and to the United States of America. An exodus of people was happening throughout the Caribbean. It is a movement that persists to this very day. Anguillans were one of the smallest numbers leaving the area at that time. During the 1950s, 1960s, and 1970s, the lines to ships and planes loading persons migrating from the Caribbean islands were always very long. At times, the exodus seemed unending. However, as I came to realise in 1955, until the actual encounter occurred, few of us planning to make the move really bothered to contemplate how strange and daunting the experiences in the new lands could be.

Probably, it was the powerful, haunting, and overpowering memories about home in the Caribbean, and the meaning those experiences brought back to them, which enticed Harry Belafonte and Irvin Burgess to write that vivid, mournful song about the Caribbean area and Caribbean life, entitled, "Island in the Sun." During the 1970s, when the West Indies cricket team toured England, that was the song which greeted West Indians at home, early in the morning, as they tuned in to hear the ball-by-ball commentary. The song is in praise of life in the Caribbean, as Belafonte and Burgess knew, loved, and remembered it. But in time they too up and left. The song's lyrics and solemn music still enchant and attract the attention of Caribbean people abroad and at home, each time it is heard. It brings back very precious memories to all who ever lived on a Caribbean island:

This is my island in the sun
Where my people have toiled since time begun
I may sail on many a sea
Her shores will always be home to me.

(Chorus)
Oh, island in the sun
Built to me by my father's hand
All my days I will sing in praise
Of your forest, waters,
Your shining sand.

As morning breaks
The heaven on high
I lift my heavy load to the sky
Sun comes down with a burning glow
Mingles my sweat with the earth below.

I see women on bended knees
Cutting cane for their family
I see men at the water-side
Casting nets at the surging tide.

I hope the day will never come
That I can't awake to the sound of drum
Never let me miss carnival
With calypso songs, philosophical.

Over time, there has been so much shared agreement with the cultural memory and yearning in this song, that it has virtually become the anthem of Caribbean emigrants. Many Caribbean migrants who hear the song still pause and go back in time to see living pictures of their earlier experiences in the islands. Then, there are those, too, who when they hear the song, join in and sing along. Others shed a quiet tear because of all the vivid memories and emotions the lyrics bring back to their lives. The lyrics are so very haunting; and speak truth to so many West Indians.

Notwithstanding those deep feelings and relived experiences from sentimental reflections, I had to accept reality. I was no longer in Anguilla. Despite the fact that the trip was an unceremonious one for me, I had promised my parents to spend at least five years in England. It was an unwritten contract. Accordingly, I had to endure the cold, the culture shock, and everything else emanating from my ignorance about life beyond Anguilla, as I settled in and learned the nuances about life in Britain. My first few days were spent taking in the vast differences between lifestyles in Anguilla and in England. Maybe it was my youth, but although there were myriad of challenges, I was quite prepared to adapt and survive living in England. The capacity to accommodate the changes was not beyond me. Rather, the challenges were part of the learning process for me. I had to remain curious and find out things for myself. Whatever the challenge took, I was prepared to grow from a cautious, uncertain youth into a confident and independent man.

For a time, I was taken-up with the change in the climate, particularly how the autumn leaves were falling, and there was also a bleak, damp fogginess as I curiously walked the streets. Tried as I might, I could not explain the dust rising from the streets at every step I took. Later someone explained to me that the dust was really black ash, which escaped from the chimneys of the houses. In time, I became amazed at how the days were becoming noticeably shorter. During October, darkness happens in England much earlier than in Anguilla. All these differences were new to me. They held my attention and challenged my curiosity for explanations.

As the weather got colder, I had to purchase appropriate clothing and I began to anticipate seeing snow. I was coming from an Anguilla I knew, to a land of different and strange weather patterning that I did not know. Accordingly, snow became something I really wanted to experience. It was one of the weather phenomena we could have talked about in the Caribbean, but never experienced. For Caribbean people who had not travelled to the colder northern or southern climates, there was very little consciousness about what falling snow is like. So, that absence of any prior experience with falling snow kept me very curious and expectant about seeing my first snow fall.

It was like a special Christmas present, when I experienced my first snow on December 24, 1955. However, when I saw snow for the first time in my life, my ignorance and curiosity led to peculiar concerns. I did not know what snow was made of. I did not know how I would be affected if I walked in the snow. And, I also wanted to know what would happen if I rode my bicycle in the snow. Here was another situation where my growing up with different cultural experiences limited my knowledge, but heightened my curiosity. It took me some time before I could be convinced that the snow that drifted down from the sky with grace, as it blanketed the ground and everything it fell on, was generally harmless as it came to the earth.

Since I arrived in England in October, within a short time I was afforded a very revealing look at the fluctuating British weather. From time to time, the shifting conditions also challenged my tenacity and almost forced me to re-think my promise to live in England for at least five years. During such times, I too reached back in my mind to the weather I knew. I thought about what my friends and relatives would be doing back home in Anguilla. I also thought about what I could have been doing in Anguilla if I was there. Then, I too, contemplated on the emigrants' anthem: Island in the Sun! However, I was no longer home.

Many years have now slipped by since I set out from Anguilla, boarded the ship *S. S. Uriga* in St. Kitts, and made that eleven days journey to England. I have had a long time to reflect on the experience, and I still do so quite frequently. My leaving Anguilla for Britain was much more than a physical journey from one place to another. It was also a journey into a challenging, strange new world where I became like a child again, encumbered by curiosity and driven to learn about a world I had never seen before. It was another world I simply heard of, and was not even certain existed. The whole emigration experience challenged my physical being and desire for personal survival. It also become a profound ideological and philosophical experience, forcing questions I am still trying to answer about human life experiences in general, and about my life in particular.

As I remember and reflect on life in Anguilla, one question I ask frequently is, "What would life for me have been like, if I did not agree with my parents and opt to make that journey from Anguilla to Britain?" I look back at my brothers and sisters; I look back at my many persons we had as friends, too. Some stayed while others emigrated from the island. For many, time has been cruel; but for a number of us it has also been very kind. . In every case, life deals a different set of cards and each of us plays them in a unique manner. The question as to whether one was a good elementary school student, is not all that matters through the years. There are always other factors to take into account, in the shaping of what one becomes. Experience taught me that as human beings face the vast ocean of life, especially when traversing the rough seas of cultural diversity, it may not be what one has already learned that becomes the most crucial factor influencing survival and success in life. It may be more a function of one's capacity to learn, to adapt, and to develop a balanced, responsible moral and ethical self, as he or she walks the path of life.

Thomas Wolfe wrote the book suggesting that in the vast complex of our experiences, once having left home, no one can truly "Go home again." It is not possible for one to go back home to the same experiences, and live life exactly as it was before he or she migrated. This is a simple, but interesting philosophical viewpoint about how migration experiences can impact and change one's life and being. Today this reality has become a dilemma, not only for the individual, but also for Caribbean societies. Thomas Wolfe was dealing with a question many Caribbean emigrants in England and elsewhere must have asked themselves again and again. If I go back home, will I experience life as I knew it before I left? Wolfe concluded that the answer is, "No!" It is never possible for one who leaves home, then return after a period of absence, to have the same experiences he or she once knew. We simply cannot go home again!

Consequently, the cherished memories I hold of Anguilla today are just that—cherished memories. I can go back to Anguilla, but as Shakespeare noted, no one can relive life that is past. It is one of those things that cannot come back to one's reality. So, time and circumstances have changed for both me and Anguilla. I go back home but many of the people I knew are no longer there. In many cases death the leveler has had its unrelenting way. Emigration, too has been persistent. Some of the places I remembered changed to a different picture from the one I hold of them. Eventually, I am left to conclude that since I left Anguilla, some fifty-six years ago, both the island and myself have changed in profound ways. Ultimately, people and the places where they once lived can lose their synergy and congruence. Nothing remains the same. Eventually, everything becomes a victim of time and change.

Once I landed in Southampton, and after I had seen my first sights of Britain, I was quickly taken-in by the many differences I noted, from the life I lived and knew in Anguilla. I soon realized that one important challenge before me was to strategise, build a plan for survival, and then find my own way in the strange land. I had set out on a new journey in my life, and I was determined, if I had the will I could find a way. Maybe others could have helped me achieve clarity and focus on my journey. However, it did not matter how others helped me, since ultimately, I had to find my own way and create a unique path to traverse in Britain. That would be the critical test of what I brought with me from my Anguillan heritage; a test of my ethical fortitude, and a test of my mettle as an Afro-Caribbean man.

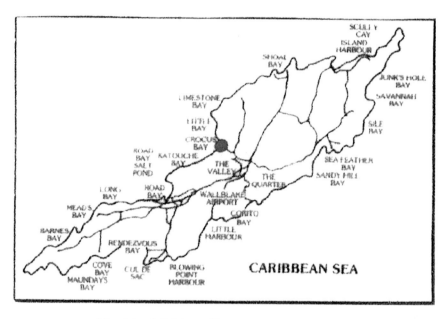

The Island Of Anguilla W. I. Where I Started.

I was born in this picturesque cottage

My Boys' School Anguilla

My present house in Anguilla

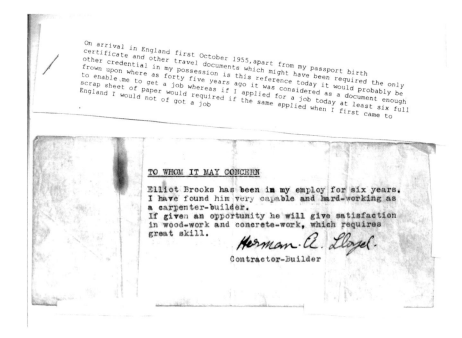

On arrival in England first October 1955, apart from my passport birth certificate and other travel documents which might have been required the only other credential in my possession is this reference today it would probably be frown upon where as forty five years ago it was considered as a document enough to enable me to get a job whereas if I applied for a job today at least six full scrap sheet of paper would required if the same applied when I first came to England I would not of got a job

TO WHOM IT MAY CONCERN

Elliot Brooks has been in my employ for six years. I have found him very capable and hard-working as a carpenter-builder.
If given an opportunity he will give satisfaction in wood-work and concrete-work, which requires great skill.

Herman·A. Lloyd.

Contractor-Builder

My Recommendation From Anguilla

Chapter Three

Finding My Way in Britain

Once I arrived in Slough and made connection with the person waiting to meet me, I started to become even more curious about my new place of abode—a country I heard so much about all my life, but started to discover I knew so little about. First I had to deal with the culture shock, then find a steady job, and in time, arrange my own accommodation—an important part of finding my way in England. However, during the 1950s, finding housing in Britain for Afro-Caribbean people was not an easy matter. Often, the process was quite a tedious but interesting task. Even when flats were available for rent, some of the landlords were concerned about the acceptance and reaction within their communities, as more and more West Indians started to move into the neighborhood. Often, there was open hesitation about renting to Caribbean immigrants. While the situation of racism was widely known, attempts were made to treat it quietly and carefully. Quite often, the situation was hardly discussed since there was the sense that it should be held as a tabooed matter within the society. The English, who had boasted about their adventures into other people's country, were quite squirmish when some of those persons started to venture into England. Consequently, the accommodation for West Indian immigrants remained a social problem "hidden in full sight" throughout Britain for a long time. Notwithstanding the inconvenience, thousands of expectant persons kept leaving the Caribbean for England on a regular basis. Britain had exploited them, kept them in a persistent poverty, and dwarfed their lives for hundreds of years. Now, thousands of those people were turning towards Britain, searching desperately for employment, a better life, and the adventure they dreamed lay beyond the islands of their birth. However, the greeting from many Britons was not always welcoming. Enoch Powell and his supporters were classic examples.

Unfortunately, during the prior contact in the Caribbean, many West Indian people had been taught to accept certain demeaning levels of social deference when dealing with white people, particularly those from England. Meanwhile, black people living in Europe from about the 1300s and in Britain from as early as the late 1500s were still being alienated by British citizens. Increasingly, Britons were forced to deal with blacks, close-up for the first time, when West Indians started to move to England in large numbers during the 1950s. The experience was traumatic for both people. Neither the British people nor the West Indians made an easy transition back to normalcy. There were many emotional scars left from that experience.

Finding comfortable accommodation was not very difficult for me. The owners of some flats at 38 Lewings Way, Cippingham, Slough had the courage to accept black people as tenants. As this information was passed around in the immigrant, West Indian community, another problem developed. The apartments were soon overcrowded. Quite often, there were other flats advertised as vacant apartments, but there was the added phrase… At other times, one would see an advertisement, and on the person's arrival to make arrangement and rent the apartment, he or she would be told that the apartment had been rented recently, and was no longer vacant. To check for the forthrightness of that situation, I once got a newspaper friend, who was white, to try renting the same apartment right after I was told it was no longer vacant. Just as I thought would happen, my white friend was invited in and offered the apartment for rent. Some landlords expressed their resentment more vigorously. They simply slammed their doors shut in the faces of inquiring West Indians. Such behaviors were quite a challenging experience for those of us who had come to see Britain as a bastion of equal rights, justice, and freedom. We had so much to learn about class and race in the real world of the 1950s to the 1970s and on.

At that time, there were more Asians (Indians and Pakistanis) in Slough than West Indians. When they realized that the British landlords were discriminating against West Indian tenants, the Asians seized the opportunity to become landlords and openly rented to West Indians. With Asians opening up their homes to West Indians as lodgers, the problem of finding places to live became less of an issue for West Indians immigrating to Britain. Meanwhile, to live in one's own flat, or in one's own rented house, allowed for certain small privileges. These included matters such as cooking meals, the privilege of having a glass of Stone's Ginger Wine, or a glass of Ruby Port on Sundays, and the freedom to develop a West-Indians-in-Britain bonding.

After some years, West Indians also started to purchase their own homes. The experience allowed us to live more comfortably, particularly as we raised our children. However, such an experience also had the scope to be deceptive. In time, the comfort, contentment, and ease the second and third generations of West Indians came to experience, belied the fact that at one time being on the bus and finding housing could be traumatic experiences for immigrants in Britain. Every West Indian who lived in Britain during the 1950s will agree that there is a vast difference between then and now. Generally, the society today is much more accepting to West Indians and their culture. We too, have become quite acculturated.

Back then, many of the working-class Afro-Caribbean people who came from the islands to Britain had been socialised to accept second class treatment on their islands. That was particularly true as they interacted with lighter-skinned and better educated persons. Consequently, at first, there was little open criticism from many immigrants about their treatment, even though they were being discriminated against by British landlords and other members of the society. Despite such challenges, many West Indians were determined to rise above the odds successfully. They were committed to a new life, to becoming survivors, and to help provide successfully for families back in the Caribbean. In my case, getting a job, eventually building my independence, and finding my way were very much on my mind. I wanted to make quick money then return to Anguilla in the sunny Caribbean to settle down and show my brothers and sisters that despite their criticisms about my education, I made it in life.

On arrival in England, apart from my passport, my other travel documents, and my birth certificate, the only other credential in my possession was a reference written on my behalf by Herman A. Lloyd, a contractor in Anguilla. The reference from Mr. Lloyd pointed out that I had worked with him for six years and that I was a competent carpenter-builder. As I reflect on that time, I now realise the recommendation from Mr. Lloyd, sent from Anguilla, and typed in black and red ink, did not really mean much in Britain. However, it did show that I was serious about getting a job in my area of competence. It also suggested that I wanted to start work as soon as possible and that I came with some work experience. As fate had it, however, I did not have to wait very long for a job. And my first work assignment in Britain was not as a carpenter. I thought the weather was too cold for me to work on the outside. Further, since I was new to the society, I simply accepted the first job that came my way. It mattered little that it was all strange to me and beyond my usual areas of competence. But, it was a job — just the thing for which I was searching.

I arrived in Britain on Saturday, October 1. The next day being Sunday, church was on my mind. I brought my faithfulness to the Methodist Church from home in Anguilla, where I attended church regularly with my parents. Even as I was about to leave St. Kitts for England, I willingly attended a quasi farewell service at the Methodist Church at Basseterre. Then, since we arrived in Britain on a Saturday, I thought it was quite appropriate, and a good thing, that I attend church in England on October 2, 1955, my first Sunday in the country. Despite the crippling sea-sickness I experienced on the ship while we sailed to England, we all arrived safely, so giving thanks to God for a safe arrival was in order. Accordingly, I located a Methodist church and went to participate in the service. The entire congregation was welcoming, but two young ladies sitting in the pew behind me showed unusual interest. At least, I wondered about the attraction because they seemed interested in me and kept picking at my jacket in the manner that woodpeckers would do. When the service was over, I turned around to face them and found out what about me was attracting them. My ego was shattered when the ladies reported that they were really plucking fluff from my jacket. Since I was a young man far from home, such a situation where I believed I was the target of amusement left me feeling uncomfortable. It occurred to me that I needed to build my confidence and exercise a greater sense of independence. I could not allow the strangeness, or the newness of place, to undermine my goals.

One of the plucking girls was Ann, the other was Sandra. While the incident surprised me, I was not really bothered by it. Further, since there were few young men in the church, it was a strategy for instant communication among the three of us. We continued our friendship during future visits to the church. However, it became obvious that some of the older ladies were not pleased about our growing friendship. Some of those ladies went on to express their dislike openly. Notwithstanding, the position taken by the older women did not deter Sandra and Ann from communicating with me. Later they were even pressured by their parents and the police. Not even such actions hindered our friendship. It persisted until I was called up for national service. Five weeks of physical bashing and no chance for contact killed that friendship. Ann went on to get married and build her family, but I still remember her as a genuine friend and someone who reached out, despite the social and cultural odds. It was also a time when I really needed a friend.

At the end of that first Sunday service in England, I was flooded with questions about myself and where I was from. During the questioning, some senior members of the congregation, Mr. Gordon Long, an employee of Western Biscuits, and Mr. Dyson were very concerned about the acceptance and integration of the late Alfred Gumbs and myself, into the church. A third person, a Mr. Shaw, was more reserved and business-like. When he spoke to us, his words were very carefully chosen and inspirational. There were two other persons whom we knew about, but they never met or spoke to us. They were Mr. and Mrs. Wright. Their demeanor was one of superiority. The fact that their daughter spoke and associated with us as members of the Cippingham Methodist Church did not help in the matter. To make things worse, their daughter eventually married a West Indian.

In general, the senior men enquired whether I was interested in employment. They noted that finding employment was a very important issue in the area and much time was spent talking about that matter. Once Mr. Dyson understood that I was in need of a job, he shared details about his workplace. He also proceeded to set up a job interview appointment for me at the Bricefield factory, in Maidenhead, where he worked. Two days after, just fifteen minutes into the interview at Bricefield, and only three days after arriving in England, I was offered a job. I took it joyfully without any hesitation.

The Bricefield engineering factory where I got my first job offer was a foundry that manufactured industrial machines. There were two sections to the factory, and the first section processed the cast iron through the furnace. Melting the cast-iron required a great amount of heat. In the second section, the processed cast iron was poured into moulds. Much of the work was done while one knelt in black sand. Further, the material used in the processing made it a very dirty job. I was fortunate to work beside Mr. Dyson who was an expert core maker. Preparing the cores for the moulds was a much cleaner job, but one still knelt in sand that looked like brown sugar. Working with the core and moulds also exposed one to some heat, but it was not as intense as that required to heat the cast-iron furnace.

I did not get the carpentry job Mr. Lloyd and I anticipated when I left Anguilla, but I was learning my new job fast and enjoyed working with Mr. Dyson. Unusual jobs such as that done by Mr. Dyson required special techniques and skills, and back in that time, specialists such as Mr. Dyson did not pass on those special skills to other workers readily. They were treated like trade secrets. However, Mr. Dyson took the time to teach me as many of his special skills that he could. Soon, I was assisting Mr. Dyson in performing a number of his duties. As I learned to manage the skills on my own, it became possible for me to do Mr. Dyson's work assignments in his absence. Unfortunately, at that time he was not keeping very well. Mr. Dyson was experiencing frequent bouts of illness and was often away from the factory. However, I was a quick learner and picked up the job skills fast. Usually, I was able to perform the work during the times when Mr. Dyson was ill and away from work.

After it was made known that I could fill in for Mr. Dyson, it began to cause some conflict in the factory. Some workers, who were at the factory many years before my arrival, thought that I was too young and too new on the job to be allowed to have such responsibility. Probably, there were also those who thought I was too black to hold such an important position in the factory. The foreman, in particular, seemed perturbed when I performed certain assignments in Mr. Dyson's absence. On one occasion, a rush order came in for a special core, but Mr. Dyson was out sick. The foreman was in quite a quandary. He went from worker to worker to see whether anyone could complete the work in Mr. Dyson's absence. Seemingly, he forgot that I was one of the workers at the factory. He never asked me. The foreman was at the point of panic when someone suggested that he asked me to complete the work. Only then was I approached and given an opportunity to lead the job. I did. To the foreman's surprise, it was done according to all the specifications and on time.

That experience with the foreman of the factory was among my first experience with blatant forms of discrimination because of my colour. It also happened again under other circumstances. Whether it was in business, in the British forces, or elsewhere in the society, doubts were always raised about the capacity of Afro-Caribbean people to perform effectively. Unfortunately, the myth that colour was a limiting factor to one's intelligence had been a factor informing British social thought for a long time. It became institutionalised by the growth of capitalism and colonialism after the 1500s. Through the years, I quietly observed responses to that incompetence myth, as I worked and interacted with a broad range of the British society. Another interesting observation I made was that during the 1950s, men were paid according to their age, not according to hours of work, or their ability to perform. I also recall that back then jobs were plentiful and easy to find.

I was very comfortable working with Mr. Dyson. However, some of the other workers acted as if they thought Alfred Gumbs, another West Indian from Anguilla, and myself were not human beings. Mr. Dyson, on the other hand, became a dear friend. He was very accepting and treated me kindly. Without any solicitation on my part, Mr. Dyson went out of his way to teach me secrets of the trade, which were rare but useful. It soon became obvious that many of the other workers, including the foreman, were not happy about the special relationship that developed between Mr. Dyson and me. At one point, some of the younger workers appeared to have been planning an attack on Mr. Dyson. Meanwhile, Gumbs and I capitalised on the myths they contrived about us. We threatened that we would eat them alive if they touched Mr. Dyson. They backed off from him. They appeared so horrified and fearful of us. Over time, while I never heard some of the other workers say derogatory things to me or about me, I often felt resentment from the manner in which they dealt with me. Shortly after Mr. Dyson died, I opted to leave Bricefield factory and took a job in Slough. That job allowed me to work much closer to my home.

The relationship that developed between Mr. Dyson and me was like that of a father and son. He was a kind man who did not display the prejudices so evident among the other workers. My friendship with Mr. Dyson was one of the reasons why I came to enjoy working at the factory. Also, while I worked as a core maker for my first job in England, I was careful to start learning about the country, and to develop strategies I could use to help me find my way, and survive in my new home.

As I recalled, there were many challenging experiences I had during that time. Some of them I will never forget. For example, I still remember my first encounter with thick dark fog. There were times when it became so dense that the whole place was darkened, forcing the factory to close early. There were some days, too, when the dense fog prevented buses from running their normal schedules. When that happened all the workers were forced to walk home. On those occasions, my biggest fear, as I trudged home through the fog, was to make it safely across the bridge over the River Thames. I also recall being so disoriented after plodding seven miles through the fog that I had difficulty finding my flat. It was such a strange and frightening experience for me.

For me, it was also quite an experience travelling the seven miles by bus to work. Sometimes, the bus was a double-decker. Often, when the bus got to my pick-up point, it would be almost full with other passengers, most of them white. Whenever I got on the bus, seating was a problem. If I sat next to a person, he or she would get up, push past me, and stand for the rest of the journey. After some time it dawned upon me that none of the white passengers wanted to sit in the seats next to me. Even if I managed to get on the bus early, the seats beside me were left open. It did not matter how long I remained on the bus, no one would sit beside me. Since I was new in Britain then, such behaviour seemed very strange to me. At first I saw, but did not understand what was happening. Because I grew up on Anguilla such blatant forms of discrimination were new to me. However, I experienced that peculiar behaviour on the bus for many months. Over time, the situation did make me very uncomfortable and quite insecure. Ironically, back then a British person would never have been treated with such indignity on any Caribbean island, and certainly not in Anguilla. If such attitudes are depicted in the Caribbean today, it is often a reaction to what has been learned about race and cultural behaviour, after emigrating beyond the islands. Despite how I was made to feel each time I boarded a bus, I continued to use public transportation to my job. . That experience did not demean me or lessen how I felt about myself. Rather, it served to strengthen my resolve, as an Afro-Caribbean man, finding my way in Britain. Maybe those experiences became part of an inner force that challenged me to step up and live up, despite all I saw around me!

Shortly after I began working in Slough, I bought a bicycle on the hire purchase plan and was given two years to pay. It cost me thirty-seven pounds. Simple as that act was, it gave me a sense of freedom and independence. I rode my bicycle to work and was able to spend more time visiting friends. Back in the mid-fifties, the bicycle was a popular form of transportation to work for many persons among the working class in Britain. Buses and trains were used more for travel from one city to another. Accordingly, I used my bicycle regularly to visit different areas in Slough. However, when I moved through places other than the city centre, there were indications from some of the persons I passed, that they did not appreciate my visits to their area. Again, since I never experienced anything like that in Anguilla, at times, I found myself struggling with the alienation which I began to feel. During that time, there were five black men living in Slough. I knew two of the others.

My work assignment at Slough was quite different from the first job I accepted in Britain, working at the factory with Mr. Dyson at Maidenhead. Since Slough was an industrial town, there were many job opportunities. I accepted a job working with a timber and plywood merchant, Danvis Bros. The firm manufactured packing cases used when shipping equipment. Because of my work experience in Anguilla, this type of work was more in line with what I was good at doing. While I enjoyed the exposure to new experiences while I worked with the machinery at the Bricefield factory in Maidenhead, I felt much more comfortable working at my new assignment in Slough. There were also new woodworking techniques that I learned over time. Also, once I managed to grasp the new work strategies for the industry, I found the experiences challenging enough so that it was like working at a new trade. Despite my familiarity with related work in Anguilla, there were many new things I had to learn. Some aspects of the operation involved carpentry skills different from anything I had seen or done in Anguilla.

I was twenty-one years old, becoming good at my second job since I came to England, and just about to get a promotion on the job, when something I never dreamed about before happened to me. Documents came with a call for me to enter the British military. However, I was naïve to such matters. I learned later that once a citizen lived in England for two years, and was within the correct age range, that person becomes eligible for national service. Because I enjoyed working at both my jobs and was adapting well to British life, I hardly realised that two years had passed by, as quickly as they did. Interestingly, prior to the official notice that I was eligible for national service, the military was the last matter on my mind. My interest in the British national service requirement came only after I received my call.

While I was not against doing national service, I was coming from tiny Anguilla, where the closest I came to martial service was the Boys' Brigade at my church. I also remembered that back about 1943, I saw about ten men on the island, dressed in a brown uniform and participating in special military training on Anguilla. Men on most British Caribbean colonies were allowed to volunteer for service during the Second World War. Then, in 1945 when the ended, there was a ringing of church bells throughout the island. Since Anguilla was part of a British colony, like all the other Caribbean colonies, it was required to prepare men so that they, too, could assist in the defence of Britain, the "mother country." When the war ended, as citizens of the world, we too rejoiced and rang our church bells.

When I received my call to national service in 1957, it was the first time I experienced real fear since I arrived in England. Suddenly, I was forced to struggle with the fact that soon I would no longer be a civilian. I was about to enter the military and become a real soldier. For me, it would no longer be something in the movies. At no point in my planning and searching for a way forward did I see being a soldier as an avenue to my future development. Soldiering was never part of my strategy to survive and make it in Britain. Becoming a soldier and serving in the British Army were thrust upon me. After the initial contact, it took a while before the formal processing of all my military documentation was completed. During the interim, I kept working at Danvis Bros., in Slough, and as one can imagine, kept thinking. I was almost driven into a daze over what to expect, and how being a soldier in the British forces would affect my life. Eventually, the call came asking me to report to the Hilsea Army Barracks at Portsmouth. On my last day as a civilian worker before I left for the army on February 4, 1958. I was just a few days short of my twenty-third birthday.

It was just past my second year in Britain and there was still much to be learned about my new home, but I was beginning to find my way. While my academic preparation in Anguilla did not set me up for a scholarly journey in

England, my other experiences on the island and in the workplace did prepare me well for the work assignments that I accepted. Despite the fact that I never worked in a factory, the experience of working and learning from Mr. Dyson was something I will always remember. We were strangers to each other in a number of ways. He knew about factory work but I did not. I was from sunny Anguilla, but he was from cold and dreary England. Mr. Dyson was an older man. I was in my early twenties. However, despite the wide ranging differences between the two of us, Mr. Dyson and I were still drawn together. At the time when our relationship developed, I was new in the country. It was one of the very vulnerable periods in my life. I needed a job, a mentor and a friend to hold my hand, and someone who could provide me some guidance. Mr. Dyson became that friend. He was my teacher and mentor. He became a special force in my life as he taught me new things and helped me to set my life on the path towards survival. As I learned new things from Mr. Dyson, he became instrumental in helping me grow as a human being. Also, looking back today, I have to admit that Mr. Dyson was one of the persons who really became an inspiration to my life. Here was an older Englishman who saw something worth nurturing in a young Anguillan. So, he worked to challenge and guide me towards finding myself and my way. While so many others I met in Britain at that time seemed insecure and selfish, Mr. Dyson was confident and secure enough to reach beyond our cultural and other differences to assure me we still shared a common humanity.

Even as I reflect today, I continue to see Mr. Dyson as a very special friend he was such a unique and different individual, when compared with many of the other persons I met in Britain. Shortly after he died, I no longer had the desire to continue my work assignment at Bricefield. For me, if Mr. Dyson was not going to be there any longer, being at Bricefield was not worth the stress the experience of being there would continue to cost me. I enjoyed what I did there, but I was able to find work in Slough, within walking distance from where I lived. Further, at that time, I found work related to what I knew I could do—carpentry.

While those early experiences of discrimination in England, as I drove on the bus to work, did not daunt my spirit, they did entice my curiosity. At first I was uncertain about why the behaviour was being displayed. What I was exposed to at the Bricefield factory also heightened my interest in the social dynamics of work relations within work organisations in Britain. Since I came from Anguilla, I was more aware about class conflicts based on one's social status. However, such a blatant pattern of discrimination against someone because he was of a different race seemed very cruel to me. Despite such experiences, I was never daunted or afraid. Over time, I was able to use those very experiences to help me find meaning to my life as I searched to find my own way. Over the years, one of the questions I have asked myself many times has been about Mr. Dyson. At a time when a large part of his society was so uncomfortable around persons of another race, how did it happen that he failed to exhibit the same insecurity? Even when Dyson was being threatened by his fellow workers, he never flinched from reaching out and treating me as another intelligent and competent human being with a great capacity to learn and grow. He took the time and patience to teach me what the others were certain I could not learn.

Another truth I learned the hard way, based on my experience with Mr. Dyson, is the inherent weakness of stereotypical behaviours. When human beings create stereotypes, they are always imperfect categories. Everything or every person in a universe cannot be included in a stereotyped description or selection, because of the experience some persons have had with a select group. Consequently, when such situations occur, the person or persons doing the labeling should be aware that the experience or behaviour being assumed to be all-inclusive, is inherently flawed because of personal biases. Usually it is far from what the persons perceive it to be. In my case, when I was being discriminated against, if I had become angry because of what happened on the job, or on the bus, and concluded that all white persons are bigots and haters of black people, I would have been very wrong. Mr. Dyson did not relate to me in such a manner. His example was the case of someone dealing with racial and cultural differences very differently, and with an unusual sensitivity... So too did my white friend, from the newspaper, who agreed to apply to landlords in Slough, who told me their apartments advertised as vacant were suddenly rented after I applied. There were other positive experiences, too. They could never all be negative, even when some people would like to categorise them that way. A number of incidents in Slough were for me early models of race discrimination. After those experiences, I also had an abundance of good, positive encounters with other white persons. When I reflect on both experiences taken together, I can do little but stand behind the conclusion that stereotypes are incomplete, mythical pictures based on personal subjectivity. Further, it is a shallow human weakness, not a strength, when people create stereotypes to humiliate and hurt other persons. They refuse to see uniqueness and diversity as a survival patterning among human beings. Actually, scientists are now seeing cultural diversity as a creative factor in human development and success.

I also learned that the survival factor was an important feature in the life of Caribbean immigrants in Britain. Usually, that desire to survive presents itself as a force to keep on, despite overwhelming odds and challenges. That was what helped me to learn new things quickly—the survival factor. It made my life evolve in important, positive, and unprecedented directions. Over time, I also developed the capacity to survive by adapting to the new environments in which I found myself. It was necessary that I understood them, learn from them, then, change quickly to survive challenges from the experience of changing environments. Seemingly, the more powerful the survival will, the more readily one learns, adapts, and grow. In retrospect, within my first three years in Britain, my life experiences soared beyond my own expectations. I even started to forget those initial plans, to make some money in England, then return home to Anguilla and build a house.

Despite the strangeness of the new environment, the survival force within me kept pushing me on so that I adapted to the weather, the stares, and the alienation. Although they both required new skills, my performance in the two jobs that I held was better than average. Beyond the workplace, I also grew in my understanding of the cultural and social nuances of Britain. Meanwhile, I built relationships with groups from varied countries and cultures—a skill that has become very important for survival in Britain. The country's earlier success in empire building, today makes it a mecca for people it once dominated and kept underdeveloped. Over the last sixty years, these people have also become powerful gregarious and integrative beings, today, an important force in British society and culture. It is a timed and contemporary product of that other time when an enterprising dominant Britain went to where these people were. Now, some of them have found their way to Britain.

Ironically, many of these people opted to relocate in Britain, so that they could escape the poverty Britain left in their islands and countries as it built its empire. Today's colonial presence in Britain remains a poignant reminder of the time when the name "Great Britain" was said with awe and a haughty pride. But, as one placard carried by a Jamaican woman in Britain read in the late 1970s, at the height of Enoch Powell's anti-immigrant campaign: "If you did not go there, we would not come here!"As noted, it's part of the timed product of British colonial domination around the world.

Interestingly, while the British went to the colonies with military power, bent on creating glory, and satisfying growing capitalist desires, we came to Britain from the colonies with a certain humility. We wanted to be accepted and integrated into the society while we helped to build Britain. Despite our varied origins, we grew up all our lives knowing we were British. Many of us made the trip because we wanted to work and contribute to the glory that was left of Britain. And, like the British of yester-year, we too were inspired by capitalist desires to search for the good life, profit, and material success. But it was no longer being realised in the underdeveloped colonies. The good life had shifted to the "mother country" and fate had her open her doors to us. Accordingly, despite our many different accents, dictions, and versions of English, we too were creatures of Western Civilization, and all aspired to speak the Queen's English. We also shared, in a general sense, respect and admiration for the British Commonwealth, and for Queen Elizabeth II.

As I moved around England, it was quite a joy to see in person those special features of Britain's geography, society, and history that I read about in school. These included the trains, of course, Lords Cricket Grounds, the Thames River, London Bridge, and Buckingham Palace. Visiting, seeing and experiencing these things about England helped me to know the country better, while I established a good sense of place location. Whenever I return to the Caribbean, I can and do speak about them knowingly to adults and children who enquire.

At no point in my effort and desire to find a path in Britain, or in life on a whole, did I consider becoming a soldier. Up to that time there was no place for soldiering in the plans I was creating. Such discipline, such a daily dance with death, and the austere life with which it is associated, were never an attraction for me. Consequently, when I got a call to do British National Service in 1957, the notice shocked me. Actually, I was somewhat uncertain for a time. From all that I was able to gather about soldiers and soldiering, after receiving the call, I kept wondering whether I could survive the experience. I knew hard work because I did it in Anguilla. I knew what it was like to be sick and really laid-up. I had that experience travelling from St. Kitts to England. But soldiering, I did not know and I was becoming very curious about it. What should I expect? How would I handle the experience? Would I survive the challenges to talk about them afterwards?

Those were some of the questions I began to ask myself. However, I began to imagine that nothing I experienced in Anguilla, or in the short time since I had been in Britain, really prepared me for my national service experience. Generally, I was correct. Meanwhile, my recourse was to steel myself, find out all I could about national service, and get ready for the call. Further, since I anticipated the experience of soldiering to be very grueling and different from anything I had done in life, I trusted God to take me through it safely. He alone knew how to help me, and could take me through such a valley of the shadow of death, if that became my soldiering ordeal. For a twenty-two-year-old Anguillan, it was no mean step in life to move from a carpenter to a soldier—and having no real idea where I was going. However, as I promised, I was committed to finding my way in Britain, and in that vast ocean of life that lay before me.

Chapter Four

From Carpenter to Soldier

My national service as a member of the British army began with a six weeks training program at Portsmouth, starting February 8, 1958. The recruits were divided into specified units and housed in the Hilsea Barracks. For me, coming from Anguilla and being new to Britain, my entry into military service began as a very skeptical journey. Because I came from the Caribbean, I knew very little about military life. I recalled that back in 1945, while I was a boy, I saw some men in uniform going through training routines in Anguilla. It never occurred to me that thirteen years later I would be called on to wear the same uniform. I even wondered whether my mother would have agreed to my coming to England, had she known that I would be called up for compulsory military service with the British army.

On my way to the training centre in Portsmouth, I first had to find my way to the Brookwood Railway Station in Surrey. I was reminded about my arrival in England, almost three years when I had to find my way to Slough, after landing in Southampton. This time, however, finding my way was easier because by then I had learned so much more about getting around by train. However, the journey in 1958 did not find me as enthusiastic as I was, when I made that first train journey in 1955. Accordingly, I followed the instructions given by the military very closely. Despite the fact that other young men were making the journey, I found the trip from Waterloo Station to Brookwood Station to be a very daunting experience. It was lonely, too. Nothing I encountered, nothing I heard, nothing I thought about, as I travelled to Portsmouth, brought me comfort, or eased my anxiety. The fact that other young men were aboard the train heading for the same destination did not soothe my tension either. It was obvious that I was not the only person who had been summoned to national service. Suddenly, we were all asked to drop whatever we were engaged in and begin a new experience as soldiers. It was the turn of our generation to take the baton, as defenders of our country. Since Anguilla was a colony of Britain, technically, Britain was always my country. At least, while I lived in Britain that question was settled. I was entitled to do national service.

All of us were on our way to becoming soldiers, but each with his different dreams, expectations, and aspirations. None of us really knew where the journey would take us. For me, it was a very long journey from Waterloo Station to Brookwood Station in Surrey. Even before I had one day of training, I started to become aware that being a soldier can at times be a very serious and lonely experience. Those were samples of my thoughts, as I journeyed and reflected on my life up to then. Meanwhile, the train snaked, rumbled, and screeched as it made the journey to Brookwood Station for the start of my life as a soldier. Suddenly, I came to realize that this, too, was another venture in Britain. I simply needed the will to endure its challenges. Even in the military, I wanted to learn the path then find my way. Despite the challenges, I wanted to step up, and as my father advised me to do when I left Anguilla, "Make sure you better yourself."

Someone was to meet the recruits at the station in Surrey, but I knew nothing about the routines on becoming a part of the military. A sergeant came along to the station and was part of the greeting group. He introduced himself quietly to all the incoming recruits. Shortly after, in military style, he began to shout the names of all the recruits from his list. And he did say John Brooks! Once the count was over and the men had gathered their equipment, we all piled into a three-ton truck and were driven to the barracks in Portsmouth. On arrival at the barracks, all civilian clothing was taken from us and replaced with military uniforms. By the end of that first day of military life, I had no doubt whatsoever that my life was about to change in fundamental ways. Everything we did was done at a rapid rate and at double one's normal speed of operation. I was assigned to Company B for my first training experience. The other recruits were divided into two other companies, A and C. Each of the companies had its own team commander, two lieutenants, a sergeant, and a few corporals. After the introductions, one was set in his team for the next six weeks.

Each recruit was issued with clothing, bedding, a bed space, then, we were given a military hair cut. At no point did I see anyone being babied in the military. It was a rough welcoming experience at my first military base. This was not a place for the weak-hearted. Day one on base was very disruptive to one's normal state of equilibrium. There was the harsh unfriendly welcome followed by long waking hours, sometimes staring at the walls and wondering what the next six weeks of training would be like. Then, there was that haunting question in every recruit's mind, "Will I survive the challenges I am about to face?" After a time, the instructors allowed us to get back to the dorms to make our beds and prepare for tea. I wondered whether they were tiring, but it was probably their way of setting us up for the rigour that was to come the next day. During tea-time we learnt something about what we should expect in the future. It appeared that with the unusual haste of the new soldiers, some of the China mugs distributed to us were chipped, as we tossed things around and panicked, trying to fall in line with our new military lifestyle. We were also in a hurry to organise ourselves. However, chipped mugs were not allowed for use by recruits on our base. Consequently, a number of us had to purchase new mugs the next day, after inspection, since new soldiers with chipped mugs were penalised by the quartermaster. There were also penalties from him for having dirty mugs and cutlery once they had been issued. On day two, everyone got an injection that seemed to knock him out after the medicine went through the body.

The next six weeks of my experiences were daunting, but also transforming. Military training challenged every sinew in my body, pushing me to the edge of sanity. There were also those times when I wondered why I left the calm security of carpentry, the beaches, and the warmth of Anguilla for such experiences in Britain. I still recall some days when merely looking at the rugby field where our first training sessions were held caused me to wet myself. Quite often, my fingers were very cold and painful. My body was still adjusting to the weather conditions in Britain. However, none of the instructors was sympathetic to me or to anyone else. They growled, glared, and shouted at us constantly. You were made to run everywhere. The training was difficult since everything one did had to be precise. Having physical strength and the ability to endure were valued. Marching and turning were only a small part of the training and there was no place for flaws. Even as one tried to be exact, understanding there was no room for error, the instructors shouted, abused, and corrected. For them, something always seemed to be wrong with what we did. Military training included intimidation, toughness, and the building of a determination to dig deep into one's inner self in order to survive it all. It broke me down, rebuilt me, and made me a new, stronger, better organised, and more purposeful John Brooks. At no point did I find the soldiering experience to be a place for weak-hearted persons. How I survived it all I am not quite certain, however, I found the guts to survive the experience. My father back home in Anguilla would have been proud of his John.

Somehow, I always had the capacity to learn fast and to grow from new experiences. Over time, I became very adept at dealing with the order, the discipline and the rigor of military life. It ceased to be the unmanageable monster I once thought it was. Not all the recruits in my batch were committed to withstanding and surviving the rigourous demands of the military experience. A number of them left the training compound without proper permission, and went absent without leave (AWOL), only to be subjected to even harsher punishment on their return to the base. Food was always plentiful. A soldier could choose from thirteen different meals every day. Each was considered to be nutritious and of a high standard. At the end of the shouting, the stress, and the humiliation experienced during training, there was food—lots of it to comfort you and probably console you until the next time.

There was one particular event at the base, which I will always remember. It came about during the sixth week after my entry into the military as a member of B Company. At first, we did not understand the instructions or realise it was intended that there be a competition among the three companies into which we were grouped. From the start of the training, the recruits had been divided into three companies. During the third week of training, we were notified that at the end of the initial six weeks of military training, the company which proved to be the most adept and most efficient at soldiering would receive the shield awarded for being the best squad in that particular intake group. The announcement about the winner would be made at the passing-out parade at the end of week six.

After that information was shared, the instructors who were initially seen as demons, started to be looked on with a little more sense of their being human beings. Suddenly, every team wanted to win the competition and be named champion company at the end of the six week training period. However, whether winners or losers, the knowledge and experiences gained during that first six weeks were a very important to the foundation of skills we would all find useful at points during the rest of our lives. As fate had it, my unit, B Company, won the shield as best all-round performer throughout the training period. Despite the challenges of the training experience, all fifteen of us stuck together, gave it our all, and soared above A and C companies. As a group we learned so much and watched ourselves being transformed in six weeks from being undisciplined rooky soldiers to competent fighting men. All the other recruits were from Britain, and there I was from lowly Anguilla. The island had no recent history of soldiering and none of the other soldiers heard about Anguilla until they met me. However, we worked together very well as a team. The end result reflected our commitment, our determination, and the synchronised rhythm we developed during the six weeks we spent working together. These factors helped us to win the trophy. It was a rough six weeks together, but in the end, it was worth the experience.

Having completed military training, we were assigned our initial postings as soldiers. It was considered fortunate when one received a posting abroad immediately after training. However, that was not my experience, for my first posting abroad came four years later. On leaving the Hillsea Barracks at Portsmouth, I was assigned to the Deepcut Training Establishment at Camberley in Surrey. It was a much more relaxed assignment when compared with the six weeks of initial military training and being initiated into the soldiering life. However, the rigid military discipline of the British army remained the same, throughout my military experience, and it did not matter the assignment. Unlike some of the other new soldiers, I was not assigned to a trade. I was assigned as a regimental policeman, so I became resigned to the fact that the assignment would last for just two years. My assignment as a regiment policeman was with the Provost Staff. My senior officer and supervisor in the guardroom was Under-Sergeant R. W. Wilcox.

Being with the regiment police was not my turn, or an opportunity to discipline others, as it had been dished out to me at an earlier time. The discipline in the guardroom was to be carried out as was instructed by the manual of military law. However, there were times when for one reason or another, the rules of the institution were ignored. As much as was possible, I stuck to the book, and probably came off at times as an inflexible and harsh guardsman. My commitment was always to the highest morale. Usually, I acted without any malice or ill feelings towards those under my charge. Despite my known impartiality, however, I was called, "Bastard," "Basil Brush," and eventually just "Basil." The name "Basil" stayed with me throughout my twenty-six years in the military. There are times when I simply look back and smile at it all, as the memories flood back. No doubt lingers in my mind that the military provided me good, invaluable, and unique experiences that I could not have received readily from elsewhere.

Notwithstanding the eventual benefits, at times I do recall my hesitancy when I was first exposed to the idea of soldiering. Back then, the idea had me somewhat intrigued, but not excited. Maybe I was even more anxious about the experience than many of the other recruits were. Most of them were familiar with it, and some shared the British military tradition, since there were relatives who served honorably in the forces before them. For me, coming from Anguilla, I heard about the military but I was not a part of any military tradition. None of my contemporary family served in any military that I knew of. We shared a tradition of hard agricultural work in what by then had become a harsh, sunny Caribbean. However, once I joined up with the military, I became committed to doing nothing but my best at everything. My thinking was that if those born in Britain could accept the challenges and do what was required of them, I could do it all, too. The message I kept speaking to myself, even before I joined the military, and during my entire tenure in military service, was, "I have to do well in Britain." It did not matter where I found myself or how difficult the challenges were. My parents wanted me to do that; and I promised my father that I would "better myself in Britain." He expected that of me.

Today I say without guile, hesitation, or with favour in mind, that having been a soldier in the British army has probably been the most important life-changing experience I have had in my total lifetime. First, the military took a very naive John Brooks, reshaped me physically, and disciplined me in a way that few other experiences could have done. When it was all over, no longer did I have an unfocused, undisciplined struggle with the forces that impinged on my life as I found my way. On leaving the army, I was much better prepared than I was before to deal with the challenges of life. It had become easier to set out and find my own paths, as I made my way through life. I was an independent thinker, I felt secure; and I knew what I wanted to do beyond the military.

When I was called for national service, my original intention was to serve in the military for the minimum period of time. However, in time, the experience of being a soldier grew on me. Then, with some persuasion, I was enticed to change my mind and become a professional soldier, travelling to foreign lands, serving queen and country, in a number of places beyond Britain and Europe. I particularly enjoyed my stints of service in Germany, Hong Kong, and Singapore. Unfortunately, I missed out on that special assignment, when Britain sent soldiers on a peacekeeping venture in my home island, Anguilla, in 1969. There was an ongoing internal conflict between Anguilla and the central government on St. Kitts over governance. While there was no major military conflict, eventually the Anguillans did win an important psychological and political war over St. Kitts and its leader Robert Bradshaw, in a continuing tug-a-war within Caribbean colonial politics.

It was during my service in the military, during 1974, that I fell in love with endurance walking for competition. At that time it was a growing competitive sport in Britain. Over time, I was able to combine the sport with bringing recognition to the British military, my desire to raise funds for various organisations that were in need, and the opportunity to win some personal accolades. Endurance walking was also something that fitted well with the discipline and toughness of military life. It was also a competition that could be done almost anywhere. The number of walking events I became engaged in, around the world, still speaks about the sport's attraction to me. Actually, I was so obsessed with the event that I challenged myself to win titles and leave my name as a champion of the sport—a feat I did accomplish eventually. The experience of endurance walking also taught me that my coming from tiny Anguilla was not a hindrance to my accepting the challenge to become a world champion. The military helped me build my stamina, confidence, and the discipline to keep going, even as I saw others falling along the wayside. I was programmed to stay strong, to keep pushing forward, despite the difficulties, the pain, and at times, despite mounting odds between my failing body and the number of miles left to go. My years as a competitive endurance walker left me with many cherished memories about the military and also about the people and organisations on whose behalf I competed. Often I stepped in on time to help them get donations so that they could meet the needs of disadvantaged persons seeking assistance. I can still see pictures and remember how my wife and children travelled around the world to be there for me. They offered support for my every effort. Truly, I could not do it all alone, or do as much as I did without them. Then, it all came together because of my experiences in the military.

Without the military as part of my life's story, I would have never caught on to competitive endurance walking in the manner that I did. I would not have had the discipline, or the confidence it took to push me on and forward, to make me a winner. Neither would I have built those special athletic linkages and friendships, nor receive the recognition as a champion athlete—a recognition that I still cherish and hold dearly. I also remember and continue to appreciate the camaraderie I experienced and enjoyed in the British army, particularly those times when I was involved in walking competitions. There were so many persons in the army who came to support me, especially from my own unit. It did not matter whether the competition was taking place on home-ground or away. There were always soldiers and civilians who came out to serve as pacemakers and drivers - we became a brotherhood. Quite often, having those others there meant so much to me. It gave me the impetus and the will to go on because others were there who understood the stress from pushing the body beyond its normal limit, but they were depending on me to see the challenge through. My wife was there, too. She would offer words of comfort, drinks to keep me hydrated, and she would always remind me about the children, as if to suggest, "Do it for them, too!" During such times in the military, serving my country my competitive activities allowed me to do things which benefitted the civilian community. Also, having those special opportunities to challenge myself, made them wonderful years that brought great joy to my life.

At my initial experience in the army, I agreed to serve for three years. Later I changed my military contract opting to serve for six years instead. However, that was not the end of it because I changed again and agreed to serve for another three years making it nine years. Later, I changed the length of my stay in the armed forces again, because the experience continued to grow on me, and because I was enjoying it. My final agreement was to serve in the military for twenty-six years, much longer than I ever intended to do national service. When I joined up at age 22, the military was never a dream of mine. But over time, it grew on me in ways I could not have imagined. Sergeant Wilcox, a regular with the army, was also very persistent in his effort to get others remain in the army, making it a career.

After some time, the sergeant and I became such good friends that I baby-sat for him every now and then. I was also able to visit his flat at the married quarters, housing reserved for career soldiers who were married. During one of my visits to Sergeant Wilcox's place, he really sold me on doing soldiering as a career. He talked with me about the perks and all the other benefits one can receive on becoming a career soldier. That included a free house, which was completely furnished. If there was any breakage, the exchange came free of cost. Wilcox highlighted other benefits, too, but I still hesitated over making the decision to become a career soldier. However, the sergeant would not accept a "no" for my answer. Accordingly, he invited my then girlfriend, Audrey, to his house for a weekend. He worked on her and he worked on me until we both agreed that becoming a regular with the army was really worth the try. The changes from three years, to six years, to nine years, then to twenty-six years, represented the hesitancy, the enticement and, the conflict I experienced, as I struggled with that matter. But, I came to enjoy soldiering, and that lessened my uncertainty as to whether I should make it a career choice. I was still very much a soldier in 1976, when my name appeared amongst the Queen's honours list for an award of the British Empire Medal (BEM). Even today, I remain proud of that honor, largely because I was selected out by my peers to be recognised for my service in the military, and to the community.

However, not all soldiers took to national service the way I did. Many of the young men who came to the army left suddenly. At times they did so without permission. They went AWOL, again and again. Others got themselves in trouble over the rules and regulations. Many young soldiers had problems surviving the harsh discipline, the austerity, along with the physical and psychological demands life of the army. Usually, the men who went AWOL were soon picked up by the civilian police and kept in cells until it was arranged for them to be escorted back to their units. They were then punished in accordance with Military Law and the Queen's Regulations. Accordingly, they would be subjected to detention or the restriction of privileges, which could range from periods of seven to twenty-eight days, depending on the severity assigned to the offence. Whatever the sentence given, there was an assignment of supervision during the detention. Quite often it was in my assignment area since being a military policeman was my usual assigned duty, and I worked in the guardroom.

My first foreign assignment came in 1962, four years after I entered the military. After that, I considered myself privileged, since I kept moving around in the army and did not stay for too long in any one place. Over time, I also reasoned that being a career soldier was almost like being a civilian. The experience grows on you and becomes comparable to the routines in civilian occupations. There were times when routines seemed almost like going to work at a factory or an office. One big difference was that the tasks involved were of a military nature. There was also constant preoccupation with military readiness and the types of duties not usually seen in the normal work-day at the factory or office.

One special assignment that I still recall vividly occurred in 1982. It involved the preparation for a visit to the military by Queen Elizabeth II. Her visit was to a military unit in Donnington, but other units, from elsewhere, were invited to the event, and to participate in the special display for the occasion. At that time, my unit was the Army School of Ammunition and we were one of the units invited to do a presentation for Her Majesty. During his preparation for the visit, our commanding officer held a series of meetings to discuss some strategic plans for the event. However, although I was the company's quartermaster sergeant, I was not invited to attend any of the meetings. Further, some of the tasks that I usually performed were taken over by the commander, or assigned to other soldiers. At that time, the British army was involved in a war against Argentina over the Falkland Islands, and it was difficult for the units to find some the munitions needed to participate in the special display for Queen Elizabeth. Most of the equipment used for such a display had been shipped to the Falkland Islands. There was even a shortage of tents to house the display. At that time, a desperate request for munitions was made to another unit whose commander was an old friend of mine. When he and my commander discussed the emerging situation, he inquired of my commanding officer, "Have you consulted Brooks?" The response of my commander was, "Brooks is new and I am not sure of his capabilities." To that response my friend retorted, "Well, I think Brooks is the best man in your unit for such an assignment." It was then that I was brought in to help prepare for the Queen's visit and invited to attend the preparatory meetings. Once I got an idea about what was required for the occasion, I told the commander that he should not worry because I would take over the planning and handle everything. His response to me was, "Fine, but if anything goes wrong I will have your head for garters." My reaction was a confident smile because I knew where to get the equipment needed for the display.

All eyes were now focused on me because what I set out to do looked impossible. There was only a short time left. Notwithstanding, I engaged the canteen and museum ladies to decorate the seventy-foot long marquee. The tent was carpeted and everything was put in place for the special day. I barely slept the night before Her Majesty's visit. Actually, I was reluctant to get into bed since my accommodation was some distance away from the venue for the display. Eventually, I went to bed shortly after midnight, but awoke by 3 AM. During the early morning hours, the heavens opened and rain poured constantly for hours. One can imagine how disappointed I felt after all the hard work it took to set things up right. Undaunted, I got out of bed early and walked to the field where the ceremony was to take place. The carpet was rolled back to keep it dry. Later, I secured some heated blowers and used them to suck up the water. Then the carpet was laid out again to make things ready for Her Majesty. At some point during the early morning, the commanding officer was awakened by his wife to hear the sound of pouring rain. Later, he reported that his wife became assured when he said to her, "Don't worry, Brooks is there." He was right!

I was delighted that he came around and trusted my ability to handle such a small matter well. Everything was done to ensure that he was not disappointed. My unit was allocated an initial ten minutes for its performance. However, our display was so impressive that we were allowed to go beyond that time. As a result, some of the other units did not get their performances done. Afterwards, I was invited to meet Her Majesty at a garden party prepared for her by the host unit. There were some three or four other times when I participated in parades where Her Majesty the Queen was present, but that was the first time I had been introduced to her. For me, it was quite an honour meeting face to face with Her Majesty Queen Elizabeth II. In retrospect, that privilege, too, was offered because of my achievements as a soldier in the British Armed Forces.

Over time, a good friendship did develop between the lieutenant colonel, commander of the unit, and myself. At times, I was even invited to his house for tea. When I was notified that his collection of antique furniture was falling apart, I took them and did the necessary repairs at no cost to him. Becoming a soldier changed my life profoundly. There were times when my experiences back in Anguilla seemed so remote and so far from what I had become.

However, when I took those chairs and used my carpentry skills to repair them, it suddenly dawned on me that the human life is one whole, the product of interconnected and varied experiences. Our past learning does not just disappear. We can retrieve and build on, or use it, directly and indirectly over time. Even as I saw myself being transformed from John Brooks, the Anguillan carpenter, to John Brooks, the British soldier, I realised it was happening to the same person, in the same body, and within the same lifetime. It did not take away from what I had become when I slipped back into my former self, to be a carpenter again. However, it was interesting that I had become a soldier and was repairing that furniture for my military commander. Actually, it was a joy for me to move back and relive that time, to discover that I could still be a carpenter, while I was a soldier. At that time, however, soldiering was all that I wanted to do; without doubt, it had come to overwhelm my life by the 1970s.

While in the military, much of what I did was difficult and involved some elements of manual labour. There were times when I did not have to do certain assignments, but I enjoyed being a soldier and associated challenges, whether they were manual or clerical. From time to time I reflected on the assignments I did, and realised that my military training was largely responsible for the man I had become. I have never forgotten the words of one commanding officer. We were in the field for a number of days and had weather that was cold and damp. At the time, I was also very tired. However, when the mail arrived at 0200 hours, despite my exhaustion and the miserable weather, they woke me and suggested that I had to work with the mail. The idea was that I moved to action immediately, since no one knew what would happen later. That was the attitude with which we operated in the military. Over time, it also became the philosophy by which I operated in, and later beyond the army.

In retrospect, there was sense and truth in the officer's thinking. Admittedly, I was angry when the idea was first proposed to me. I now look back at that stance taken by the commanding officer, nicknamed, "Beak." He deserved and earned our respect for his professionalism and leadership qualities. After some time, I was also inspired to follow in that officer's footsteps, seeking to pass on and share positive ideas with other soldiers and civilians alike. The result was that just as my commanding officer did, in his time, I too, gained the respect of my fellow soldiers as I passed on my knowledge and experience helping to impact their lives in positive ways.

I had a long and relatively secure period in the army. However, the time did come when I began to contemplate my return to civilian life—a place where I would lose the protection, structure, and order I experienced while serving in the military, but I would be in charge of myself. It was never my intention to work for anyone, but myself on leaving the military. The problem was, I had no idea what I should do with my life after the army. Accordingly, I spent a number of months browsing through newspapers anticipating that something would catch my eye and attract my fancy. Eventually, I saw and was attracted to an advertisement about how to start up one's own business. Once

I had reviewed that information, I was much better prepared to launch out on my own. Because of my experiences as a military policeman, I once thought of becoming a private detective. I also contemplated merchandising, since it would not require major initial capital outlay if I kept it as a small operation.

Business involvement was on my mind when I packed, said my good-byes, and walked away from the military, on March 24, 1984. It hardly seemed that long, but by then I had spent almost eight times three years in the military. One of the many things for which I was very grateful to the British army was that it allowed me to participate in many charity walks. Those occasions were also situations when I experienced the camaraderie of the varied units and felt appreciated. There were individual soldiers, the pacemakers, and all the drivers who lent their services to aid and ensure my success. Such experiences stood out as memorable reflections about the years I spent in the British military. They did me well psychologically. Twenty-six years were much longer than I thought I could survive there, but it was twenty-six years that I will never forget. They transformed my life. They re-wrote my story. They also changed the dreams I once dreamed and saw as destiny. No longer was I limited by that "duncy" label with which I left Anguilla.

Chapter Five
Soldiering in Strange Lands

After completing basic training, my first assignment was at Camberley in Surrey. However, during the 1960s, Britain still had wide-ranging colonial influence and ties in the Caribbean, Asia, and Africa. In every one of those places dominated by Britain, there was a haunting evidence of poverty. Notwithstanding, there were military bases in places such as Hong Kong, Singapore, Malaysia, Cyprus, and Aden, for example. The British also had bases in Europe, Canada, and Africa. Many of the Caribbean islands were also still British colonies. At some point, all soldiers, particularly the new ones, looked forward to an assignment in the colonies, or to some base overseas, beyond Britain. For me, it took four years before I received my first overseas assignment.

The assignment came in 1962. The posting was to the Seven Ordinance Field Park in Germany. For me the move meant that I was separated from my wife and best girl, Audrey, but I remained very excited about the opportunity to have my first assignment abroad. The Ordinance Field Park (OFP) was an active unit that supported a brigade. Accordingly, we kept ready to move, as necessary, at very short notice. Despite the unit's need for constant readiness, we had an enjoyable social life there in Germany. The only special requirement was that we be back at the barracks by 23.59 each evening. Alcohol was cheap and there was always female company around. I took time to learn about the local people and spent quite some time with them. Audrey was not with me, so I had to find ways of occupying myself when I had time on my hands and was away from duty. I also took the opportunity and time to start learning the German language.

Another soldier named Greg teamed up with me and we devised a system by which we worked on learning the new language. When Audrey did manage to join me in Germany, I was confident enough with the language so that I could visit shops and do purchases on my own. As one can imagine, it was quite a show-off for me to go shopping with Audrey and be able to speak and translate the German language. Most of my experiences in Germany were good ones and I enjoyed being in the country. I also found the people to be quite friendly. Their festivals such as wine tasting, cultural dances, and accompanying costume displays interested me and gave me opportunities to be exposed and to learn about their different culture forms. The Germans always made us feel welcome. One of the dances I enjoyed was usually performed at functions held by the local policemen. After a night out on the town they would have their annual ball in a well known guest house. Some of the other soldiers and myself would gate-crash the event, then take over the activities as many of the policemen continued to drink until they were drunk. Usually, their wives sat nearby and looked on helplessly. I had two years of soldiering in Germany then it all came to a sudden halt. During 1965, the orders came for my assignment to Singapore in the Far East. I t was my second overseas assignment, time hardly appeared to have slipped by so quickly, but there I was a British soldier being sent on my second assignment overseas, ten years after my arrival in Britain.

Our 24-hour flying journey to Singapore began at Heathrow airport in London on a carrier called the British Eagle. We boarded the aircraft and were sitting for about one hour when a voice came over the public broadcast system stating that there was a problem with one of the engines. We sat and waited until the problem was resolved, but no one was happy about the delay. Eventually, we were on our way to Singapore. As we passed over the Indian Alps, the aircraft dropped suddenly, again and again, and shook repeatedly. After the sudden frightening experience above the Alps, we did land safely in Singapore, about two and a half hours later. Our group was met at the airport by Sergeant Jim Tomkinson, who took us to a hotel. We stayed there until a house became available for us.

When I compared Singapore to what I knew of Britain, and what I saw in Germany, Singapore was not the cleanest place that I visited up to that time. However, we found it to be a shopper's paradise. One was at a further advantage if he were skillful at bartering. The island was very hot, but we had access to a swimming pool. It was later observed that Bougie Street doubled as a shopping centre during the day and an entertainment centre during the night. Singapore was also noted for its red light districts. Most of the soldiers would attend regimental functions first, then while still dressed in uniform they would head for Bougie Street. We also discovered that Singapore was linked by road to Johore Barroo in Malaysia. Shopping and entertainment in Malaysia were also very good, so we made that trip many times.

While in Singapore, my assignment was as a store-man. I purchased sporting equipment for the unit and ran the rugby club as well. At that time, like many of the young men with whom I had been stationed, I was no angel. Further, I was in the military and very curious about such matters of the world, as would entice young soldiers at that time. I took my chances, got a myriad of experiences, and satisfied my curiosity. Most members of my unit, including myself, left Singapore with very fond memories of the area.

As we prepared to leave Singapore, it dawned on me that the years had flown by quite fast. It was 1968, but hardly seemed that thirteen years had gone by since I left Anguilla. Suddenly, I was experiencing a yearning to return home. I wanted to visit the Caribbean again. There was an inner yearning to see Anguilla. I also sensed a longing to spend some time with my family members still on the island. However, I had some initial problems gathering the air fare. During my time in Singapore, despite keen interest in the culture, the shopping, and all the other different experiences, one benefit from being stationed there was that I saved money from my extra allowance. Finally, I had the funds needed to travel back to the West Indies. Accordingly, I applied for leave with the intent of visiting Anguilla in 1968. However, my request was turned down because during that period there was ongoing unrest between the central government in St. Kitts and the people of Anguilla. Because Nevis was a part of the three-island colony, Nevisians too had been drawn into that drama between St. Kitts and Anguilla. Soldiers were stationed at a military outpost on Nevis and on the ferry between St. Kitts and Nevis. All the other Caribbean islands looked on with interest. Eventually, Britain, as "mother country," reluctantly entered the colonial mêlée of the time to help search for a resolution to what had been a long festering colonial problem. Prime Minister Harold Wilson of England responded by sending British troops to Anguilla, March 19, 1969. His intention was to restore peace and order within the Caribbean colony. Robert Bradshaw, then leader of the islands, was quite disappointed that Anguilla was not forced back to his overlord-ship with Nevis and St. Kitts.

Some weeks later, after my initial request to travel to Anguilla had been turned down, I received a letter indicating that conditions in Anguilla had improved. It was then possible for me to proceed and take my overdue leave. I was excited and enthusiastic as I responded to the order granting the leave to travel. I was very excited about having the opportunity to return home after such a long absence. That yearning to see the Caribbean in general, and Anguilla in particular, had become unbearable. So, my tour of duty in Singapore ended and I wanted to go home, not to England, but to Anguilla. I was awaiting that moment for a long time. Soon, I would be on my way to the West Indies via England. However, when I got to the airport in Singapore, I found myself stuck again. This time the problem was not with the aircraft, a VC-10, military aircraft. The problem was related to fighting in the Middle East. Our flight-path back to England went that way, and passed over the area where the fighting was taking place. Another problem was that the British pound had been devalued and the financial world was showing a measure of instability. Eventually, the problems were all resolved. My trip to Anguilla was soon on again.

Going back home to Anguilla after being absent for so many years was a pleasant but humbling experience. There were changes from when I lived there, but they were not dramatic changes. It was more a subtlety in the experience of looking backwards in time. The island was far away from the sophistication of technology, trains, traffic overload, the order and discipline of soldering I had come to know, love, and appreciate in England. However, despite the culture lag I experienced in Anguilla then, I had gone back home to the island of my birth—the place where I grew into adulthood, a part of the Caribbean area I kept seeing in my mind's eye, and longed for, time and time again. My visit to the island on that occasion lasted for four weeks. In retrospect, they were very glorious weeks. I visited my family, spent time on the beaches, went throughout the island, and appreciated every spot along with every moment there. I savoured the beauty and enchantment of the island in a manner I had not done before. There were also those times when I simply got away from everything and watched the world as it passed by, in quaint and quiet Anguilla of the 1960s, tucked away as it were, in the calm, enticing Caribbean Sea Actually, my vacation-time passed by too quickly. It ended before I was really ready for it to be over. However, I had to get back to my real life and to the tough discipline of the British army. Accordingly, I laid down my leisure shoes, put away my Caribbean and beach clothing, and made the trek back to England. There, I put on my uniform and the accompanying boots, picked up my gun, got my orders, and became a soldier again.

When I returned to Britain, I was assigned to my third tour of duty abroad and the second tour of duty in Germany. I was sent to Bielefeld Germany and spent just enough time there to meet some of the local people and get to know the area. Due to some military reorganisation, within a short time I was reassigned to Belgium. That assignment was a short one, too. Soon I was reassigned back to Germany to a field force unit in Munster, for my fifth overseas assignment. This unit was an active unit with many opportunities for exercises. Unfortunately, the leaders in that unit were poor bosses and ineffective leaders. During my free time, I was expected to remain and cover for my boss. His supervisor was on his back. After a time, as I completed my tour, things began to change for me, but it was not possible for me to benefit greatly from the change.

The overseas assignments provided opportunities for me to move around from one country to another and to learn about different cultural nuances. However, there was no one place where I spent a very long period of time. After another brief assignment in Germany, I was shipped back to Derby in England, then to Sharjah in the Persian Gulf. That was my sixth overseas assignment.

Despite my being from the sunny Caribbean, I found the Persian Gulf to be a place that is very hot and sticky. The weather condition there also influenced the military assignments, which soon became monotonous and boring. About mid-day, a series of flags would be flown to indicate which activity could be undertaken. The dark blue flag meant that everyone should stay in the shade. However, such warnings were often ignored. Many of the men, including myself, would use the time to play volleyball. Within six months of my being posted to Sharjah, the base was closed down and the equipment dispersed carefully. I felt happy to have been involved with the process of closing the outpost at Sharjah. Many persons felt the closing was overdue when it happened.

The very hot weather was a drawback to the post, but Sharjah had its good points. It was in a desert but the facilities were excellent. We had air-conditioned rooms for recreation. There was open air cinema for those who wished to attend. Once or twice per month I could drive to Dubai, thirteen miles away. Dubai is an oil-rich state that is multi-racial and there were bars that remained open until about 10:30 PM, depending on which bars one chose to visit. Common sense made me choose the bars where British bands were playing. At an agreed time, the Sheikhs would come to the bars. That usually closed things down for us, poor soldiers. The price of drinks would suddenly shoot up beyond the range of soldiers' pay. If one enjoyed shopping as entertainment, Sharjah was the place to visit. Jewelry was cheap and gold tablets the size of a match box could be bought in open air markets. Unlike Dubai, Sharjah was not an oil-rich country.

One very special memory about my posting in Sharjah was that three days after I arrived there, a telegram came with the news that my wife had given birth to a son. For me, that was very good news. We already had two beautiful girls. That time around, we were hoping for a boy. My family grew then to be five persons: Audrey, Jacqueline, Christine, Andrew, and myself. When I left for Sharjah, it was known that we were expecting another baby. However, I never allowed my private life to interfere with my military duties. Further, I knew Audrey was a strong woman who could manage such a situation well, whether or not I was at home. . There were also other Caribbean family and friends who would lend support to her.

By September of 1971, my duties in Sharjah were over. I was on my way back to Britain to be stationed at Bicester in Oxfordshire. That was in place of the exotic assignment I was hoping for, an assignment in a place such as Hong Kong, Singapore, or some other warm place, not cold England. From all the rumours I heard, I was not excited about being stationed at Bicester. However, I concluded later that the rumours about Bicester were misleading. For me, it turned out to be a pleasant, welcoming market town that I liked very much. Actually, we were stationed at Ambrosden, just outside Bicester, and there were many country stores located in that area. It was while I was stationed at Bicester for a two-year period that I took to the hobby of long distance, competitive walking. Along with soldiering, long distance, competitive walking became the other profound shaper of my life.

At one point, in 1974, during my stay at Bicester, a letter came in to the unit from The National Society for the Prevention of Cruelty to Children (NSPCC). After that letter arrived, the year 1974 came to mark a turning point in my life. I had been searching for something new and different with which to engage myself, but I could not make up my mind about what it should be. I was very aware about my limitations in academia because I failed to make the effort and take my educational opportunities as seriously as my siblings did at school back in Anguilla many years ago. I still wanted, in some way, to achieve at a high level at something in life. I had to move beyond the limitations of grade school in Anguilla, and soldiering was nudging me there. It was now important to me that I did something beyond the ordinary so that my family, the young people of Britain, the Caribbean, and possibly the rest of the world, could one day see me as a champion somewhere and at something. I kept thinking that there had to be some way I could discover such an objective which I could pursue in life. I also wanted to inspire others, without relying on academics. But, I was not certain about which direction to take.

That letter from the NSPCC to my unit at Bicester came as an answer to my prayer. Its special request was that the unit sends some volunteers to participate in the annual fundraising event at Aintree Motor Racing Circuit, in Liverpool. It was a demanding, non-stop, four-day walk around the racing circuit. Because I was the sergeant major at the company's headquarters, I had an opportunity to see the letter. Accordingly, I approached the commanding officer and indicated that I wanted to participate in the fundraising activity. However, before the application to participate could be completed, there was a special criterion to be met. The participants had to be able to walk 75 miles in a twenty-four-hour period. The commanding officer agreed with my request to take part, but I had to do the test walk. Arrangements were also made so that I could get some media coverage.

Since I was a member of the Forty-six Shadow Company, the unit arranged to hold a twenty-four-hour walk for me around the Graven Hill Circuit. The media was invited along with independent judges to officiate at the event. I could then complete the application and enclose the proof that the 75 miles were covered. I did it, not in twenty four hours, but in seventeen and a half hours. Afterwards, a training program was set up so that I could be ready for the NSPCC event. The training routine included full-time training in the gym and one overnight walk from Bicester to Slough. The main event had been arranged for May 24, 1974. Excitement was high. Everyone including myself waited with great expectation.

I was prepared for that first event the best way I could. When the day came, I arrived at Aintree just about mid-day. Since it was my first time participating in such an event, I did not really know what to expect. We soon learned that my team was under-equipped when compared to the others. However, I had good logistical support, enough transportation, and the food was adequate. The walk began at 6: 00 PM. After forty-eight hours, a number of the competitors had dropped out. Meanwhile, psychologically, I appeared to grow stronger as time went by. On the third day, I was still feeling strong. The crucial hours came for me between 2 AM and 3 AM. During that stressful time, I began to experience hallucinations, something that I had never experienced before. The hallucinations altered the functioning of my mind, to the point that it took a considerable amount of persuasion from my pacemakers to ensure that I carried on. By daybreak the hallucinations were gone. It was day four and there I was, alone on the track. Even some of my competitors were encouraging me on. But my frame of mind was neither clear nor normal. But, I could hear my supporters as they kept repeating, "You have done it. You have done it." Accordingly, I concluded that I had covered the intended 305 miles and sat down because of the exhaustion being experienced. After the normal five minutes break, I simply refused to get up and continue the race. Later, I discovered that I had stopped some 13 miles short of the actual target. We were able to present the NSPCC a cheque for four thousand pounds as a result of the walk.

Two years later, in 1976, after having spent eighteen years in the army, my career as a soldier almost came to a sudden end, when I was posted at Brunei. Even now, I am reluctant to mention and discuss my posting in Brunei, although I spent six months there. It was a memorable, but unpleasant experience—undoubtedly one of my worst overseas tours of duty. Prior to my arriving at Brunei, I received a letter from the commanding officer for the RAOC unit, Major P. J. Temple. He suggested that I bring a fishing rod and civilian clothes. However, since I was still a soldier in uniform, despite my receiving that letter, I took my full military equipment to the outpost. I had just returned from a course in physical training shortly before being shipped out to Brunei. My assignment with the unit should have been dual. I was to serve as a physical training instructor and also the sergeant major and supplies specialist.

On my way from Baracus to Brunei, I noted a sign that read, "FETE, in aid of the Ghurkas Welfare Fund." Because of my prior involvement with such matters, I started to think that I could help to plan and organise a thirty-mile walk with and for the Ghurka unit in the area. It was a way of contributing to their fundraising. However, on my arrival at the barracks and during my first day in Brunei, I started to surmise that something looked odd. There were activities that left me feeling very unsettled about the outpost in Brunei. Accordingly, with time, I became increasingly suspicious about some the activities I saw. As I reviewed my assigned duties, I began to conclude that Major Temple and his entire crew in the unit were operating the outpost fraudulently. The whole unit was like a massive lottery system located on a sandy bank in the desert. Supposedly, four accounts were kept at the unit but none could have withstood the scrutiny of an audit. Local workers had been asked to burn the accommodation store's accounts. The two miscellaneous accounts were meaningless, and the general store's account was kept hidden from me in Major Temple's office. Gradually, I started to reflect on the strange letter that was sent before my arrival in Brunei. The way the unit was organised and managed seemed very strange.

Most of the equipment bought at the base was very expensive, so I began to ask questions of Major Temple, based on my observations. His response was to write the Records Office in Leicester. He referred to me as useless, and someone who did not get on well with the local people. Both accusations were lies. Whenever I served overseas, I made friends with the people there and attempted to understand their culture. The Records Office also knew that such accusations against me were false. They were very aware of my commitment to local communities and their wellbeing. Eventually, my experiences in Brunei led me to conclude the entire outpost was a corrupt unit, the worst and most unpleasant assignment in my whole soldiering career. Based on my observations, I simply opted not to get deeply involved with the divisive link I noted existed between the military outpost and the local populace.

Quite often, I observed that there were special invitations and offers of food. However, I was very cautious about accepting such hospitality. It soon became evident that some of the local men who came around the outpost were con men and special friends of Major Temple. Every day two men were there when we stopped work at 1PM. They took us to the bars to drink and eat, and strangely, it was all free of cost. About 4 PM, we would drift home, covered with sweat, and giving our wives the impression that we were just from working very hard at the base. The whole charade appeared to have been a strategy to get us drunk, then the men would slip their orders in for equipment from the post. One could be asked to approve up to 1000 mattresses, 500 instantly, then the other 500 at a later date. Questions about batteries and tires often came up after long drinking sessions. My soldier buddy appeared to have gained the respect and confidence of the men who followed us around, but they always seemed to dislike me.

During my first meeting with Major Temple, I was informed that whatever material was needed at the outpost should be sanctioned by him. He also observed that there was little privacy for married soldiers, since local men were in and out the barracks conducting all our affairs. Since the unit was largely an outpost, it seemed strange that it sold a large quantity of surplus stores along with vehicles considered beyond repair. The sales by the unit were very popular with the local people. However, as the situation required, I maintained records on the vehicles we sold. On one occasion, a vehicle arrived from the workshop without a number plate. When I attempted to identify the vehicle by making a check of its engine's number, I discovered that it was a vehicle we had sold previously. The matter was reported to Major Temple. He became very furious on being presented the information. I soon realised that his fury was not really about what had happened, but about being caught in his double standards and scheming deals. At one point, thousands of pounds worth of equipment was ordered from Hong Kong, but it all went to the workshop without signature. On checking the workshop's inventory, none of the equipment was there. I later concluded that the unit was not working in the interest of Seven Gurka Rifles, but in the interest of the local businesses. And it was all for cash. Vehicles that were condemned were being repaired by the workshop and sold; some vehicles were sold repeatedly. While in Brunei, there was continuous friction between Major Temple and myself. It turned out that had I not stood up and fought back against the commanding officer, his actions could have damaged both my family life and my military career. Despite the many challenges I encountered during my stay in Brunei, with the help of a British civil servant, I managed to stage a 30-mile walk in order to assist the Gurkas Welfare Fund. About twenty to thirty locals participated in the walk. They had never witnessed such an event before. Together, we raised about $8,000.00 in one month.

I saw the Brunei store section as very corrupt. It operated like a shop that served local businessmen and special sales vehicles were included. Despite my efforts to cooperate and work with Major Temple and the local people, I never met Major Temple's standard for corruption. Rather, I endeavoured to rise above all that I saw as being wrong at the base. It was not the major alone who was corrupt, so too was his senior ranking soldiers. Their scheming was costing the British Government thousands of pounds in unauthorised sales, and I could not become part of such fraud. Eventually, I requested of Major Temple that I be allowed to have an interview with the commanding officer in Hong Kong. The interview was granted, but not before Major Temple had completed his tour of duty in Brunei, and was on his way back to England.

As a result of the interview with the commander in Hong Kong, I was transferred from Brunei to Hong Kong where I finished that stint of overseas tour of duty. Hong Kong was my seventh opportunity to serve overseas. While in Hong Kong, I was fortunate enough to visit China and Bangkok. In 1976 when I was stationed in Hong Kong, it was an important British colony and military base in Asia. Twenty-one years later, that arrangement ended as the British returned the colony outpost to China in 1997, just at the turn of the twenty-first century.

My soldiering went back to normal and routine while I was stationed in Hong Kong. By then I had become well known for my charity walks in the places where I had been stationed before. Consequently, while in Hong Kong, I started to examine the possibility of doing something there for charity. Hong Kong had a number of uniformed organisations and many youth clubs, including persons in wheel chairs. My intention was to raise some money to benefit them all, but we also to make the walk a fun experience. We agreed on a twenty-four-hour sponsored walk to be done in the Hong Kong Stadium. For me, it turned out to be one of the most strenuous walks that I undertook in my career. It was an unusual event because for the first time since World War II, in April of 1978, the people of Hong Kong became interested and excited about an event organised by the British in Hong Kong. More than thirty years had passed since the British had so much publicity in Hong Kong about something they organised. The walkers were all from the Composite Ordinance Depot at Blackdown Barracks. During the twenty-four-hour period, I walked just under 102 miles. We raised 40 cents short of $46,000. 00, so I made a special donation of the forty cents. The event was very successful and enjoyed by everyone who participated in the effort. In addition to handing over the cheque for the charities and clubs, our unit also received the Wilkinson's Sword of Peace for its community consciousness while I was in Hong Kong.

My tours of duty overseas ended with the almost three years I spent in Hong Kong. It was a much warmer and more pleasant experience than I had in Brunei. Now, almost fifty years after my first overseas assignment, I still look back, with fond memories and great contentment, at the many and varied experiences I had overseas as a British soldier. During those experiences, I learnt so much that I did not know before about the world around me. I learned about its different people and cultures. I learned about my personal survival as a human being. I saw life and soldiering from varied perspectives. There was also so much I learned about myself that I did not know before. When I left Anguilla for Britain in 1955, soldiering was never on my mind. Even after I became a soldier, I wondered what the experience would be like and what it would be worth to me. Today I view my soldiering experiences quite differently. The challenge of being a soldier in the British Forces, serving in England and in countries such as Germany, Belgium, Singapore, Brunei, and Hong Kong, transformed my life. I was helped to fashion a new and different view of the world. It was during those years that I changed from being the naïve, innocent young man that left Anguilla, to a mature, aware, and disciplined man in England. The journey through my military life took me twenty-six long, tough, and disciplined years. However, they were and always will be seen as years that reformed my being and my life in unimaginable ways. If I had to live that period of my life over again, there are some things that I would probably change, but I would always go back to being a soldier.

The experience won my heart and exposed me a new and wider world. Within that new wider world, I discovered other human beings whom I came to love and respect as both family and friends. During those years, my dear wife Audrey increasingly became a force for stability and vision in my life. At the same time, our children inspired my life, giving me hope and dreams that I too will touch the future. Then, there were the many friends whom I came to know along the way. They broadened my cultural experiences and challenged me to live a life that counts beyond my home and immediate family. Quite often when I am alone with myself and do take some quiet time to reminisce, I see those times of discipline, competition, love, family, and friends, as powerful softeners, forces for wellness, and a very vibrant, meaningful source of strength in my life. I still treasure those experiences.

John Brooks- Starting out in England

Basic Trainnig-1958

Basic Trainnig-1958-3

Basic Trainnig-1958-2

On my BSA - To get around to and from the military 1958

Passing out Parade - 1958

B Company -Winners' Shield - 1958

Mj. Gen. Jackson Preship Brooks the Queen's honor of BEM - 1976

In The Seargents' Message

Met Queen Elizabeth II - 1982

Soldier and Gentleman

Chapter Six

Finding Love, Family, and Friends

As a young man growing up on Anguilla, I admired the way in which my mother and father loved, respected, and were always there for each other. It was common on Caribbean islands, that parents, back then, took the time to nurture children, both brothers, and sisters, in positive ways. Most persons growing up in the Caribbean at that time were also exposed to the extended family situation, where parents, grandparents and children formed a close survival circle and were there for one another, sharing home setting, transferring the accepted culture values, and ritual forms, from one generation to the other, through the years. That was also the reality of my own experience growing up in Anguilla. I shared that common patterning of family life common in Caribbean islands. It was also existing in Anguilla, at that time. Consequently, although I was still becoming of age in England, I often looked back to my Caribbean past for insights about love and family. That was what I knew. At the same time, I was very aware of my immediate surroundings, including the cultural differences impinging on my life—shaping the choices I made for my future life. By the time I turned eighteen, and as I got into my twenties, I too became very attracted to the opposite sex. Not long after I joined up for national service with the military, my interest in a long-term relationship also began to blossom. There is a certain loneliness experienced by soldiers and I was struggling with that feeling. It seemed to have been heightened by the discipline, the daring, and the self confidence that come together in the life of soldiers. Another factor was that I was far away from Anguilla, my family and friends - I was lonely and feeling it!

It was at that point in my life when I met Audrey Arrindell. She came to England from Sandy Point, St. Kitts, to study nursing, and was living with her aunt. I knew Audrey's aunt and met Audrey at her place one weekend. For me it was love at first sight. Soon after, I recognised the intensity and hopelessness of my macho situation. So, I let Audrey into my life and she became my forever love, partner, and woman. At the same time, there were fading dreams with which I struggled, about another Caribbean woman, one I left in Anguilla. But she too had moved on with time. She migrated to Nevis, and fell in love with someone else there, whom she later married. Audrey is still a beautiful woman, but back in 1960 she was fifty years younger, tall, stunning, and very mysterious. Instantly she stole my heart. She soon had me thinking and believing that life for me without Audrey Arrindell would not be complete, and not worth living. We moved quickly because I was confident and knew Audrey was the woman I wanted. We met in1958 and were married in 1960.

Our wedding was held on June 25, 1960. It was five years beyond my arriving in England, and I was just about two years into my career with the military. Audrey was in her final year of training to be a nurse. When she completed her training, Audrey willingly accepted the invitation to join me at Deepcut, near Camberley in Surrey. Accordingly, I applied for the married quarters that Sergeant Wilcox had shown me and spoken so much about one year before. I was claiming my perk after becoming married; however, there was still some uncertainty about whether I would agree to become a professional soldier. Actually, it was while we were on a weekend visit with Wilcox that he convinced Audrey and me that I should become a professional soldier. Once we reviewed the possibilities, we later agreed to get married, soon after she finished training. We did share my married quarters from time to time, after we got married. However, when Audrey was moving in to live, for the first time, I bought some paint to re-do the interior of the apartment. To my disappointment, Audrey did not like the colours I chose. She reminded me that pink was more a colour for the bedroom, not the living area. I also used red for the floors and for anything flat or made of cement. In retrospect, I now agree that red and pink inside an apartment were crazy colours. Seemingly, because she was caught up with the unusual pink living area, Audrey did not notice that the cooker and burner had been cleaned and made to look lovely. I was very careful to spend time cleaning them and to have those implements bright and shining, as my bride moved in to share our new accommodation.

Last year, June 25, 2010, marked the 50th year since Audrey and I got married. That has been a long time, almost a lifetime. But, God has blessed and preserved us together through all those years. We are now able to look back and remember where we have been, savour where we are today, and still dream about our tomorrows. Children came early after our marriage. We had four of them: Jacqueline, Christine, Andrew, and Andriea Marie. Unfortunately, Andriea died suddenly from crib death, not long after she was born. She was just a few weeks old. I was stationed in Germany and dropped by to see my family at about 10 PM. When I said good night to the family and left for the barracks, Andriea smiled back at me. Accordingly, I returned to the unit thinking that all was well with my family. About 0300 hours I received the call. Andriea was dead. Later, the post mortem diagnosis pronounced it to be crib death.

We had two girls before our boy came along. Despite the children, Audrey travelled everywhere with me, particularly when I went on my overseas assignments. Sharjah was the one overseas assignment to which Audrey did not accompany me. It was a short assignment and the sanitary conditions were not welcoming to a lady. However, through all those years we enjoyed our many and varied experiences together. Sharing with each other became an integral aspect of our life together. I will always remember the support my family afforded me during those many endurance walks, for which I became well known. Because she is a nurse, my wife understood well how to care and nurture me, during those many times when I was worn-out and on the verge of breaking down.

Because of my shifting assignments with the army, our children's education was interrupted every now and then. There were times when I had to place them in boarding schools, too. That was the case when it was determined the area where we lived was unhealthy for their education and development. On an average, we moved every two years, however, the family and I were not the only persons affected by the frequent moves. Such was part of the reality in military life. It was a system affecting the lives of all military personnel, at some point or another. By the time my children completed their schooling, I was out of the army and in business. This provided an opportunity for the children to get some work experience. It also allowed them opportunities to experience the dynamics of management. For example, Jacqueline and Christine worked with me for some time until they chose to branch out and become engaged in careers of their own. Later, Jacqueline worked in real estate until she developed her own handicraft business. Christine went into the fashion world. She modelled quite successfully and at one time became Miss Banbury, the area where we live in England. After some time, Christine seemed to have become tired of modelling. She went off to university where she studied criminology. Andrew was studying science at one time, but after a while he turned to music and kickboxing. Like his father the endurance walker, Andrew the kick-boxer won many titles. He broke a number of records, too.

At this time, we are more than parents. There are grandchildren, too. The two of them, Sian and Ruth, are doing well in school. While Sian enjoys horse riding and music, Ruth's interests are in foreign languages, music, and horse riding. At times when I interact with my grandchildren, I also reflect on what my life has become since I left Anguilla and came to England... Today, I can boast a good family life. The children grew up finding roots and wings in Britain, but also finding a niche there, on reaching back to their roots in the Caribbean. I also continue to hold fond memories of the many things we did together as a family. We visited many different countries, and everyone shared the rewards from my military success and my walking exploits. I also shared and enjoyed the accomplishments and successes of all the other members of my family. For example, throughout the years, my wife Audrey has been a skilled and competent nurse. The children have also had individual successes, too.

Recent developments and changes in our family include several events and situations. Jacqueline and her daughter, Ruth, have now moved to live in Spain. Christine worked for two years on contract in the U.S. Once the terms of the contract were completed, she moved to Anguilla, reaching back to her Caribbean roots. She now works there as a probation officer. Andrew bought his own house and moved to High Wycombe. He has lost interest in kick boxing, but Andrew remains keen on music. His daughter Sian lives with her mother and continues to progress well in school. It is not hyperbole when I say Audrey has been a rock of support to my life, from the time I met her, throughout my time in the military, and on up to the present time. Often, because she is trained as a nurse, her ability has been quite useful to me, to our work relationship, and to other experiences we shared together. When we ran the nursing homes her experiences in nursing were useful and very beneficial to the business.

There were times when the situation at hand required that Audrey turned to her profession, worked long hours, and put social activities aside, because these were necessary so that we overcame some difficulty, some financial limitation, or some other demand on our family. For example, there was that time when Audrey moved and joined me in Germany. She had just received her nursing qualifications and our first child Jacqueline was about two years old. Audrey was determined to fill a vacancy in the family clinic on base. Arrangements were made for Jacqueline to stay with a German family while her mother worked. Jacqueline was soon learning the German language. She also kept telling us about the many stories she saw on television.

Through the years, Audrey and my children have been there for me. We share a very useful and supportive bond. Our relationship gives very special meaning to what the word family means to me. I needed them all, through those long years in the military when there was a longing for softer, gentler, and more humane touches to my life. It was always a joy to know that I could find solace, comfort, and an unusual tenderness in the arms, heart, and life of my wife, children, and other family members. Further, it has been a very comforting and assuring experience to watch as my children grew from innocent, naïve young people, to active, mature, thinking adults. During my efforts in business, they were there with me, helping me through it all. As I reflect on the pathways my life has taken, I am forever aware that I could never have climbed the ladder I took to success, reaching the heights I attained in life, without the support and intimacy of my biological family. We worked and built dreams together. Today, I am forever grateful, forever indebted to both my children and to my wife Audrey. Meanwhile, my children and close friends who know me well are also aware that Audrey has been a steady force and quite an anchor to my life. In reflecting on how far I have come, I do not see the stability, the successes, or the survival through bad times as being possible without the love, the strength, the ingenuity, and the commitment of my

Audrey. She was there for our children and she was there for me. Quite often I saw in her actions pictures of my mother Inez, a strong, loving, innovative, and supportive Caribbean woman. As a boy, I watched and admired my mother, while she stood beside my father, and stood with their eight children. Together, my parents demonstrated fortitude, as they met the challenges of difficult life circumstances in Anguilla. It was by facing such challenges with a certain confidence that they prepared their children for change and the future. Despite a stressful situation and harsh, trying times, my parents were able to raise their eight children successfully, and to experience a relatively successful life in Anguilla.

Without even knowing it, Audrey reenacted and demonstrated the force, the strength, and the loyalty I saw in my mother, back in Anguilla. While the culture and conditions in Britain have been different in many ways, some of the challenges that faced my wife, my children, and myself paralleled those which my parents encountered in Anguilla. There was the challenge of raising children, then giving them "roots and wings" so that they too could survive into the future. There was also that subtle instability that being in the military brings to one's family life. Despite our frequent moves, Audrey was there as an anchor to the family. She provided stability and consistency to the lives of our children. Then, when my military life was over, Audrey was there for support and at times as innovator, particularly when we ventured into the nursing home business. Much more than I did, she understood the demands of the tasks involved. Audrey led out, she worked along with the rest of us. She also planned well so that the business could become as successful as it did, under our leadership. However, I must hasten to emphasise that the comparing of my wife with my mother in no way intended to limit my wife to the person, or the achievements of my mother. I simply admit to seeing a certain similarity of character and patterning in how both women dealt with life, and resolved everyday human problems. Actually, I also saw two different Caribbean women, coming to the stage of life in different eras, in different places, and under very different circumstances. They were two different Caribbean females, linked by time and circumstances, but two Caribbean persons who in their own time, left special markings on life's stage. Each of them also demonstrated a certain moral fortitude to life and its many challenges that others, particularly their children, saw and could learn from. As often as I reflect on what my life has been is as often as I have concluded, if I had to live my life over again, the person I would choose to be my life's companion, to be the mother of my children, and to be my business partner, would still be the woman I married almost fifty-one years ago, on June 25, 1960, Audrey Arrindell. She pleased me then, and fifty-one years later, after all we have survived together, she still pleases me.

Besides my immediate family, there were three other families into which my life became woven. They are my Anguillan family, my Caribbean family, and my military family. A part of my family remained in Anguilla and I have always stayed in touch with them. However, because of our very long history of migration in the Caribbean, once a native person moves beyond a Caribbean island, the family connection becomes broader than the immediate relatives. It broadens to include other natives of that island living in the new place. Consequently, my family grew to include other Anguillans in Anguilla and Anguillans who came to live in Britain. Here in Britain, we created an Anguillan Association so that Anguillans and at times other Caribbean friends and well-wishers could meet, reflect on our problems and successes in Britain, and on emerging social, economic, and political issues back home in Anguilla. Our Association was also interested in the welfare of Anguillans, and it provides common ground where visiting politicians from the islands can talk to persons with roots in Anguilla or the other Caribbean islands. Further, whenever I go back to Anguilla, I am able to find my niche and to enjoy my visit. Whether I visit alone, with family, or with friends, the whole island accepts me as one of its own. Over the years, I became so comfortable and confident about going back to Anguilla to home and family that I invited others to visit with me and experience the island.

In 1986, I took my British friends, Bridget and Barry Munson, with me to Anguilla. They, too, were enchanted by the warm family type relations they observed on the island, yet they were strangers visiting with me and my children. In reflecting on her visit, after returning to England, Bridget Munson wrote quite a bit about the experience. It was her first trip on a plane, so she was somewhat apprehensive. It was also her first time to the Caribbean area. Her many comments on the visit and about Anguilla still intrigue me. A number of quotes from her letter follow. "I did not know what to expect of the place or the people, well in a few words the feeling was for me that we all had come home." She wrote further, "We were part of the family, and down the road there was Iris and her daughter Sarah who made us very welcome. And then there was Uncle Willie Daniels, well, he really made us feel at home, and there were lots more people in the Valley and all over that made us really at home. Now that we are home, I feel that we have left our new friends such a long way away." Sarah also wrote, "I miss their friendly ways. I feel homesick for Anguilla, the place and the people who made me feel I am one of them. I hope I can go back again and again. My whole world changed after meeting the lovely people of Anguilla."

In 1998, I finally built the house on Anguilla, as I had promised myself to do, way back in 1955. In Britain, I am very much at home. However, many persons in Anguilla are my extended family, I wanted to have my own house there, and to look at the business options on the island too.

We established the Anguillan Association as early as the 1950s and it prospered for a number of years. I also accepted the challenge to do something practical to help Anguillans at home. Accordingly, I decided to help meet the cost of sending an Anguillan student to college in England. During 2004, I was granted a very special award by the government of Anguilla. It was an acknowledgement of my contributions to the development of Anguillans and the advancement of mankind. I accepted the award with gratitude and appreciated it greatly because there was the Anguillan Government acknowledging that despite the fact that I no longer reside on the island, I am still family. The award was in recognition of my continued Anguillan connection. It also showed appreciation for my commitment to the island's well-being.

In 2009, I was the recipient of another award from my Anguillan family. The recognition came from the Anguillan Progressive Association. It was given in appreciation for my contributions to, and my achievements for, both England and Anguilla. That, too, was an award I accepted gratefully because it took me back to my roots. It also strengthened my connection with the island where I was born. Despite my long absence from the island, I still go back regularly to my Anguilla and to the Caribbean. They remain as participating actors in my yearnings and dreams, since I left Anguilla and the Caribbean, back in 1955.

Associated and linked to my Anguillan family is my Caribbean family. It is a special shared link I will possess, throughout time in the area, as part of the African Diaspora on Caribbean islands, also in North, Central, and South America. That link has deep roots in Africa and the history of capitalism in these areas. I grew up knowing that Anguilla was linked with St. Kitts and Nevis, but I became much more aware of my Caribbean family during my years in Britain. Throughout my years in Britain, since the whole Caribbean area shares the common urge to emigrate from the islands, I met, shared ideas, and experienced a special solidarity with many other Caribbean people. They were Jamaicans, Barbadians, Nevisians, Dominicans, Antiguans, and more. Meanwhile, I ended up marrying a Kittitian. The girl I dated before I left Anguilla, left the island and got married on St. Kitts-Nevis , keeping that St. Kitts, Nevis, and Anguilla connection in my life story.

During the year I served as Mayor of Banbury, one of the innovations I added to the city's ceremonies had a Caribbean dimension. I introduced a Caribbean festival, a culture and style that were still strange to the area then. However, beyond Anguilla, and things Anguillan, there is a Caribbean-ness that connects us to all the islands in the western Atlantic Ocean. It is part of our peculiar history that takes us all the way back to Africa. Despite my many years in England, it has been impossible for me to forget my relationship and connections with these people. There is that common, but profound saying in the Caribbean, "We are all related. Our ancestors from Africa were simply landed on different islands." It therefore seems impossible to deny or forget my deep Caribbean and African connection. Accordingly, I do acknowledge having a forever shared connection to the other Afro-Caribbean people in the area.

For twenty-six years, I was part of the British army. Being part of the military for so long eventually made it family. Those familial relationships were demonstrated again and again, as I moved from barracks to barracks and unit to unit throughout my military career. The family relationships were further heightened during my marathon and endurance walking years. I depended on both my army family and my biological family, every time. They worked with me and make my successes possible. I never walked alone in England, in Hong Kong, or in Canada. My military family was always there along with my biological family. Together, we walked around the world. We won recognition and awards, set and broke records, together. Those experiences were very important to me. I still conclude that in doing so much for me, the military re-shaped the entire script for my life. After five years in Britain, I did not quit and return home to build a house as I had anticipated. After five years in Britain, I was in the military, married, and loving what my life had become. All those dreams I built about Anguilla, my future, and myself, had been disrupted, put on hold, forgotten, or changed, all because the army had come into my life.

As time went by, the military experience grew on me. There were opportunities to travel and see the world. I also received appropriate recognition and promotions for my achievements in the military. And I had the opportunity to push myself, to grow, and to develop in directions I never dreamed of. For example, in 1974, at a time when I was searching for innovation in my life, because of my being a part of the military, I was introduced to marathon and endurance walking. Later, as the years went by, my walking was often sponsored and supported by the army. At most of my walking events, the pacers and drivers were members of the military. Many of the friendships I developed around the world happened because of my affiliation with the army. In 1974, while a member of the military, I became the British Commonwealth endurance walking record holder, having covered 446 kilometers in four days. In 1975, I was entered in the Guinness Book of Records as a champion in endurance walking. During that same year, I had the opportunity to visit the War Office. The intent was that I create a special cassette to be used for training by the British forces in Germany. One year later, in 1976, I was awarded the British Empire Medal (BEM), and later that same year, I also received a special invitation to visit and spend a day at the Houses of Parliament. While there I visited both the House of Lords and the House of Commons. During 1982, after I participated in setting up a special display to entertain Queen Elizabeth II, I had the honour of being introduced to her. It was an experience for which I was very grateful. Through the years, I still continue to reflect on such special occasions and events in my life.,

Most of my first thirty years after I left Anguilla were spent in the British Armed Forces. Although I was married, and had a loving biological family, it was impossible for me not to become part of that big military family to which I had been introduced and became attached. Throughout those twenty-six years, the military very much a part of my life and came to mean so much to me. If I had not become part of the military family, I could not have seen the many places I saw around the world. I would not have discovered the athlete within me either. Further, it was the military that did more than anything else to put me on the stage of life as an important actor and participant. The military ensured that I received special recognition and awards, too, while I stood on that grand stage of life. It has been to me a very close and dependable family member, one I cannot forget, as long as I am alive. My Anguillan family, my Caribbean family, my biological family, and my military family each touched my life in some peculiar and special way. Then, they all found a systematic way to come together as building blocks, but found synergy in transforming my whole life. Over time, each of these four families that entered my life made an indelible contribution as they came together forging a common force, to shape and mold me into the man I am today.

Probably, success in endurance walking was one of my greatest areas of achievement in the military. It was done largely for charity, but it required discipline, martial training, and much commitment on my part, and a love for what I was doing. Over time, it became a very rewarding experience for me, in that I won recognition, set records, and became known around the world for my skill at endurance walking.

No book about my life is complete without a chapter giving broad reflections on my walking experiences within and beyond Britain. When I began walking competitively in 1974, the experience brought a new impetus for living and being, to my life. It became something that challenged my total self every time I performed, but it was an endeavour that brought meaning to my life. I had to depend on others for support, and there was always the choice to perform at my best or be humiliated by the opposition. Quite often, too, there were persons in need who depended on my effort to fulfill a need, bring comfort, and console their lives. There were also times when I broke records and received personal commendations for my endurance, my physical skills, and my extraordinary walking performances. Today, I look back in gratitude at such opportunities. I am still very grateful that they all came my way. Together, they are also tangible evidence that my emigration from Anguilla to Britain made a difference in my life, and in the man I have become.

John and Audrey Dating -June 25, 1960

John and Audrey being Married, 1958

Brothers Three

Daughter Christine, Miss Banbury 1986

John with wife Audrey

Mr. and Mrs. Mayor 2006

With wife son and daughter

Granddaughter- Sian

My Hong Kong Years

My Hong Kong Years

My Hong Kong Years

My Hong Kong Years

Assisted Anguillan Students In Britain

Assisted Anguillan Students In Britain

Chapter Seven
I Fell in Love with Walking

Sometimes, I find it very interesting to reflect on the strange twists and turns that my path through life has taken. During my early life, never did I dream that one day I would be a British soldier or visit as many countries as I did. In retrospect, those years of my being in the military became the period in my life when I discovered my true self. I also developed new perspectives on the journey of life in a way that I would not have done in Anguilla. In time, I even grew to enjoy being a British soldier. Then, during 1974, while still in the military, I was introduced to the athletic feat of endurance walking. Commenting on the benefits and the challenges of endurance walking, one expert, Dick Crawshaw, then a champion walker and British parliamentarian, noted, "The first 100 miles are physical—after that, the effort's mental."

It was an off-the-wall invitation sent to my unit asking soldiers to take part in an endurance walking event in 1974 that got me into the sport. I was in love with soldiering, but over time, I fell even more deeply in love with the challenges of the walking sport. Many readers may even wonder why I walked for such long, crazy, and mind-boggling distances. For me, the answer was always quite simple. I did it to test myself and to raise money that would help persons I saw as being less fortunate than myself. At times I thought about all the children in the world, who cannot walk, run, jump around, or who are dying from cancer, through no fault of their own. Another reason for my walking was the satisfaction I got from doing it. Contrary to what some persons think, endurance walkers are not just a few mad human beings. In 1975 when I participated in one event, there were one hundred and fifty persons in the competition. At one time in Hong Kong, thousands of citizens from various strata of society took part in a pre-endurance walk challenge. None of those long distance walking competitions was ever easy. There were always physical and mental hardships associated with such endurance events.

At times, it was my determination to succeed that helped to push me along, and kept me keeping on, despite the intense and painful physical challenges. Quite often, the severe challenges of endurance walking made me reach into myself for inspiration beyond the ordinary. It tested my fitness. It challenged my determination. And it inspired me to beat the competition. Often, I found it difficult to find the stamina, with which to withstand the physical and psychological pain, and to maintain my sanity, because of the strain the experience of endurance walking brought to my body. It soon became more meaningful to me, than the soldiering to which I had become very committed. Endurance walking took over my life and started to influence most of my daily activities. As a new interest, it became an avenue to personal growth, a vehicle to raise funds for charity, and a tool for developing cross-cultural linkages while broadening my communication with other people. Soon I became known for my endurance walking efforts in Britain and elsewhere. I also became noticed for my keen competition and commitment to charitable giving during the next eight years of my life and beyond. Today, I still take time to smile and reflect on how endurance walking came to be an important part of my life, and how it shaped my professional and personal development in the military, and in civilian life. Today, I still say without any reservations, all three branches of the British military supported my endurance walking efforts. I could not have experienced the success I enjoyed without them. Wherever I competed I could have counted on the support of all branches of the military. Now, in my mind's eye, I can still hear the shouts of encouragement and adulation as I trudged round and round in circles, that challenged my total being and took me to the edge of my sanity.

My introduction to endurance and charity walking in 1974 was sudden. I was a staff sergeant with the Royal Army Ordinance Corps (RAOC) and stationed in Bicester. The letter to my commanding officer from the National Society for the Prevention of Cruelty to Children simply invited soldiers from units based in the Bicester area to participate in a four-day endurance walk event for charity, which was to take place from May 24 to May 28. The event was new, but becoming an attractive annual walking competition. . Only fifty persons were allowed to participate in that race. Well known endurance walkers invited to the four-day walk included: Dick Crawshaw, Member of Parliament; Corporal Russ Phillips of the Canadian armed forces, also known as the Roadrunner; Jesse Castaneda, a teacher in Mexico, who held the world record for a 302-mile walk the previous year; and some others. At that time in 1974, I was a mere rooky to the event.

For me, such a diversion and new challenge came at the right time. I was searching for something new with which to engage and challenge my life, but could not decide what it should be. I also wanted something that was new and different with which to engage myself. Since endurance walking offered a new physical challenge to me, time was spent finding out about it. I discovered that there were set physical stipulations that interested persons had to meet before they could apply and participate in such events. For example, one had to prove that he or she could walk at least 75 miles in a twenty-four-hour period. Despite the physical severity of such a demand on the body, I fell in love with endurance walking immediately. I felt confident it was a feat I could accomplish. My body was tough enough, too. Consequently, I agreed eagerly to participate in my first twenty-four-hour endurance test walk. However, we first had to find an appropriate venue where I could perform the test walk. As fate had it, we agreed to use a circuit in Bicester. It became the venue for my twenty-four-hour sponsored test walk.

A number of prominent officials along with the local press were invited as witnesses to verify the distance and certify the time taken to complete the trial walk. Shadow Company organised and provided support for the event. There was no shortage of manpower. When it was all over, I had taken under eighteen hours to walk the 75-mile test distance. Following that success, my application to participate in the four-day walking event was submitted. However, I was still a novice to endurance walking, so it became necessary that I worked out and followed a training programme for my first four-day walk. Meanwhile, my unit became abuzz with excitement over its great expectation for the event. The interest and excitement were shared by the press. Notwithstanding, I kept a low profile as I worked at my training program. The army was very accommodating. It granted me special leave so that I could use the gym during the day. Most of my walking practice was done during the night. I would set off from Bicester at midnight and walk to Slough. Usually, I arrived at Slough by breakfast-time. That distance is about 68 miles. When I arrived in Slough, my wife or a relative would be in place to give me a ride back to Bicester. Not all my practice walks to Slough were done during the night, but most of them did take place at that time. My thinking was that I should not limit myself to any one formula as I trained, but that I should be versatile. Accordingly, I kept pushing myself beyond normal parameters and continued my training right up to the day before the official walk.

The four-day walk started at 6 PM. We were set to walk around the 1.64-mile racing circuit at Aintree. Thirty persons started the walk. Right from the start, I took the lead and kept it. However, talk began to spread that I could not complete the walk since I was a new and inexperienced competitor. However, there I was holding the lead, a rooky endurance walker and the only black participant in the race. Notwithstanding, I held my pace and kept listening to the broadcast system. After some time, I learned that I was ahead of the nearest competitor by eight miles and increasing my lead. When we completed the first twenty-four hours, I was about 15 miles ahead of my nearest rival. At the end of three days, I had also worn out about twelve pacemakers. They experienced problems walking because of blisters, bandaged ankles, plus hip and thigh injuries. Some simply became dead tired, burnt out, and unable to keep up. As they gave up and returned to the unit headquarters, new persons were sent out to serve as pacemakers.

Meanwhile, since it was our first walk competition, we were not as prepared as some of the other teams for all eventualities that could have occurred. By the second day of the walk, I began to experience hallucinations. The sky seemed to be just above my head and in touching distance. At the same time, the stars appeared to be lights inside buildings. The cracks in the surface of the road also started to look like a barbed wire fence, as I walked around the strip of tarmac. Occasionally, I saw images of shire horses, as I approached the benches. There was also water that seemed to move about. At other times there was the appearance of a very high fence around. It took the skill of my pacemakers to assist me in staying on my feet and moving forward. They became very good at helping me to overcome my hallucinations. Up to that time, in my short walking experience, that walk was the first time I experienced hallucinations. For me too, certain sections of the walking surface always seemed more difficult to navigate between 3 AM and 4 AM ; and I kept experiencing that difficulty until dawn was about to break. When dawn broke, my body came alive again as if re-energised by the beginning of the new day and the coming of the sun. That was my experience on more than one of the four days.

The rules for the competition stipulated that one could break for only five minutes during each hour. Such breaks were to change footwear and for other comfort necessities... Any break longer than five minutes led to disqualification. No time was allowed for eating or drinking. These conveniences were dealt with by snatching things to eat and drink as the walk progressed.

A large part of my sponsorship came from ordinary working people; somehow, they often appeared to be more generous and give more to charities than the large, wealthy companies. Two large firms gave their support, but I had a contractual agreement with them that I wore their clothing and footwear. John White Shoes of Northampton supplied the shoes for the occasion and Dunlop supplied the clothes. My wife Audrey seemed to understand very well the stress and the pain I was experiencing during the walk. Consequently, she kept me supplied with drinks, spoke comforting words, at times about our children, then, she was quickly left behind as I got back into my rhythm for the walk. Audrey was particularly useful for her advice on caring for blisters without breaking the skin. Also, her skill and healing expertise often helped to save my toe nails. It was Audrey who concocted my diet for endurance walks. The stables were jam sandwiches, hot tea, Dynamo, and Accolade. That combination of food material worked well and seemed to provide me the extra energy I usually needed.

During the Aintree race, there was one competitor whom I kept seeing in the distance. My tactic was to catch him, pass him, then catch him and pass him again, as I went around the circuit. It was quite normal; after three or four days of continuous walking, the strain of the task began to tell on the mind and it became blank. At that time, the pacemakers were responsible to keep the walkers motivated and their feet moving forward. When walkers are in such a state of mental uncertainty, it is only the pacemakers and pure will that can keep them going onward. I came to understand what Crawshaw said about the role of will and agreed he was right. One of my competitors gave up and dropped out early on the fourth day, as he experienced the severe stress the competition forced onto his body. In my case, I can still remember the loud cries as a show of massive support greeted me on that fourth day, as I moved around the motor track. Then, there were shouts of, "Amen! Amen! Amen!" from the crowd. Those were welcomed shouts which bolstered my spirit. Then I remember hearing someone say, "You have done it. You have done it." There was no doubt then that I was way ahead of any challenger and comfortably leading the pack.

At that point, I felt overwhelmed and went to sit down not knowing there were still another 13 miles to go, if I were to set a new world record for the four-day walk. By the time I became aware that my goal of setting a new world record was not met, I had already been sitting for more than the five minute break allowed by the rules and could not reenter the competition. My next stop after the four days of a gruelling walk was the Walton Hospital. I went in for a twenty-four-hour compulsory bed rest and observation. At the same time, comments about the walk and its results were being broadcast throughout Britain. Later my name was entered in the Guinness Book of Records. I had walked a distance of 289.6 miles and set a new British, European, and Commonwealth record for the four-day walk. It was my first endurance walk competition, but I was able to have my name added to the growing list of noted endurance walkers. The previous best distance walked was 256 miles. After that four days of walk, we were able to donate about 4,000 pounds, British currency, to the NSPCC charity.

Because of my outstanding first time performance, I received a number of congratulatory letters from military commanders in the area, including Brigadier-General Minogue and Major-General Stanley. The official umpires for the race, Joan Gregory and Peter Anstey, also presented me with a certificate that read: "This is to certify that JOHN E. BROOKS, competed in the World Record Non-stop Walk event held at Aintree Racecourse from 24th to 28th May, 1974, and completed 176+ laps for a total distance of 289.64 miles." A special award came from the eccentric owner of Aintree, Mrs. Mirabel Topham, also a supporter of the four-day walk for charity. She sent me a pot of homemade honey. Seventeen months later, in the 1975 race at Aintree, I managed to set a new endurance record, completing 305.4 miles in seventy-five hours. During that year, I was also awarded the NSPCC winners' trophy for my performance in the four-day race held in 1974.

Throughout my remaining years in the military, I took part in numerous walking events. They were usually done for charity, but among the individual endurance walkers, some healthy rivalries did develop. As we competed, each of us wanted to out-walk the other, to break, and to set new records. Many of us moved around to compete in special charity walking events held in Asia, America, Europe, and the Middle East. At that time, endurance walking had become one of the popular means by which to raise money for charity. Always, it was an endeavour that demanded endurance, tested one's fortitude, while it afforded entertainment and extrinsic satisfaction for the onlookers. Over time, many persons and firms became committed to making useful donations to such demanding feats of endurance. . Meanwhile, the walks always provided some ego boosting and a sense of accomplishment for the successful competitors.

Another of my memorable walks in 1974 took place shortly after the four-day walk at Aintree. An invitation was received asking that I participate in a 350-mile plus road walk. It was to take place twenty-nine days after Aintree. The walk was from Birkenhead to Plymouth. Despite the short time distance between this walk and that at Aintree, I accepted the invitation to participate in the competition. Road walking is a different pattern of walking. Here the scenery changes and there is the interference with traffic. However, the will and endurance demands are the same. Whether the walk was on a circuit, or on the road, my wife Audrey remained an important "go-to" person for me, as I pushed myself during difficult and stressful moments. Since our children were still quite young, my wife also decided to bring them along, rather than leave them with a baby-sitter. It turned out to be quite a challenging task, having the children along on the road walk. However, my wife always seems to manage well, the things she sets out to do. Audrey would arrange for the children to sleep in the car while she made herself available to provide the support I needed. She drove ahead for two or three miles then waited for me to catch up. During the road walk, we were better prepared than we were for my first event at Aintree. When I caught up with my wife, she would provide a change of socks, some drink, and some food. Once I was refreshed, Audrey moved on for another few miles until I caught up with her again. Unfortunately, that walk had to be abandoned. Shortly after we arrived in the Dartmoor area, gale force winds and very heavy rain provided a challenge for which I was not prepared, and had no defence . A fierce storm descended on us and did not let up. We experienced blinding weather condition as the sky darkened and a storm broke. The rain became unrelenting. Suddenly, the steep hills were too dangerous to climb. There were also problems with the pacemakers, the labourers, and the transport teams. Our team was too disorganized, so we I abandoned the race at Okehampton. Despite all the setbacks, a large sum of money was raised for charity. It was enough to help a young boy travel to Switzerland for assistance with a medical problem.

I cannot look back today and say that endurance walking was ever an easy game without extreme physical challenges and psychological stress. However, I grew into it, as my body made the necessary adjustments over time. Despite the demands on my physical and emotional self, my participation in such fundraising events represented my commitment to keep helping others who were in need and could benefit from such donations. There were numerous organisations to be tapped for such assistance, and to which we could make our charity contributions. In my case, they included the Army Benevolent Fund, the NSPCC, and other charity organisations that help military families in a variety of situations.

Just about one year after the road walk, on May 10 to 11, 1975, I dreamed up the idea of a twenty-four-hour walk, around the clock, in the Aldershot Military Stadium, a 400-meter track. There were eight competitors involved and all of us agreed that the walk would be purely for charity. As usual, most of the donations came from the local community. The walk started at mid-day on May 10, and continued for the next twenty-four hours into May 11. Such a competitive endeavour, then or now, is never easy. There is the physical and psychological stress of being in a competition with other men who are comrades, your equal, and with whom you are competing to prove yourself better. . Then, there is that encompassing demand to stay strong, stable, and alert for twenty-four gruelling hours of continuous walking. Even as that desire to rest comes again and again, one has to reach into the inner self to keep on. Meanwhile, it is always an important competition factor that one's back-up team is well organised and prepared to provide effective support. These are some of the persons on which endurance walkers depend heavily all the time.

Later, in August of 1975, I was back in the walk at Aintree. Because of all my activity for the year, I was in excellent shape. As a result, I felt on top of the world. My performance resulted in a new record of 305 miles for the event. However, here again I was unhappy that I ended my walk when I did. Maybe I had enough left in me for another 50 miles. If I had accomplished that, it would have put the record beyond reach for years to come. I am not certain at this time where the present record for a four-day walk is, in relation to the 305 miles I set back in 1975. After my many successful walks and donations to charity in 1975, the city of Bicester, where I was stationed, began to be seen as a place worthy of increased interest. Tourists increased their visits. I was also named as one of its twelve most outstanding personalities of the year for 1975,

By 1976, the Canadian roadrunner, Corporal Russ Phillips, and I had become very good friends. We met at Aintree, we were both military persons, and we loved endurance walking as a sport. Each of us was also gunning to beat the other. Later, I invited Russ to compete in Britain and he in turn invited me to compete in Canada. We were involved in a number of twenty-four-hour walk competitions, and he tried again and again, but he was never able to beat me. The competition in Canada was billed as a walk to aid the mentally challenged in Saskatchewan. Since the summer of 1976 was very hot, it made the walk extra tough to do. I even got sun burned, in a way that I could not recall having experienced before. At the end of the event, there were scars on my back and shoulders. The marks that were left remained on my body for a long time.

It was just before the Olympic Games when Russ Phillips sent an invitation for me to visit Canada and assist in the endeavour to raise funds for the mentally challenged in Saskatchewan... The agreement was that we participate in a twenty-four-hour walk. It was the third time we would be up against each other in endurance walking. Airlines in the US were on strike, but I was determined to get to Canada at all cost. Meanwhile, my unit was behind me and totally supported my mission and the effort it was designed to aid... The walk was to take place from Saskatchewan to Moose Jaw. Like all my other walks in foreign countries, that in Canada was both strange and somewhat different. However, I had made the commitment to travel and compete in Canada against my friend Russ Phillips and I was totally committed to that mission. I knew he was waiting anxiously for me to arrive. Despite the airline strike, it would be against my better judgment to disappoint him. Both of us also looked forward to the walk. We relished the competition.

The Sergeants' Mess in my unit paid for the flight to Canada. The plane strike did not prevent me from making it there on time. I arrived at Calgary at night, then, in the morning hitched a ride to the starting point for the walk in Saskatchewan. The ride to Moose Jaw was not a very comfortable experience. The helicopter rattled and shook all the way. However, I was treated with great respect and admiration once I got there. A red carpet was laid out for me, and the people I was about to help lined the short distance and greeted me as I walked from the helicopter. During the entire week I was there, my accommodation at Moose Jaw was provided by the best hotel in the area. It was arranged for Audrey to meet me at Moose Jaw, but the airline strike caused a delay and prevented Audrey from meeting me there. She got stranded on a Greyhound bus from the US to Canada and the trip took her six days to Moose Jaw. When Audrey arrived I had already moved out of the hotel and was at the base preparing for the event. At the new location, too, my accommodation was pleasant and impressive.

The walk in Canada was successful. We raised some $7,000.00. Afterwards, Audrey and I were given the freedom to roam throughout the city of Regina. It was another one of the twenty-four-hour races where I beat Phillips, but he was much smarter than I was during the event. Because he was familiar with the weather condition, he covered his head and shoulders for protection from the sun, as we walked around Gutteridge Fields. Instead of ensuring protection, I concentrated on building up the miles and staying ahead of Phillips. At the time, I was hardly aware of how the sun was burning my body and affecting my skin. It was after the walk, and then, for a number of days later, that I noticed what the sun had done to my skin. Before my Canadian experience, I was not aware of the extent to which the sun could damage one's skin—even that of African people.

However, I fell in love with Canada during my brief visit. The people were kind and friendly. As I experienced the welcoming hospitality in Canada in 1976, I could not help but be carried back in time to the 1950s. I recalled that the Canadians were very kind to Anguilla and Anguillans, when I was a boy growing up there, a little over twenty years before. The island had few amenities then, and most of it was donated by Canada, not by Britain. While on that trip to Canada, there were times when all our hosts had to do was make a phone call. Then, within a few minutes we could be by a lakeside or some other pleasant place having a barbeque. I was also given a number of job offers while in Canada. However, my two girls were still at boarding school in

Britain. Further, at that point I had completed eighteen years in the military, with eight to go before I retired. . There was some excitement about the job offers and the prospect of living in Canada. However, because of the situation with my children, and my time already spent in the British army, I smiled at the offers, expressed my appreciation, then packed my bags and prepared for my return trip to Britain. As fate would have it, that same year, 1976, because of my involvement with charity walks, I was nominated and received a special award in Britain. By that time, I had successfully raised some $160,000.00 for charities, because of my endurance walking

It is not that the hallucination episodes or the periods when my mind went blank made it impossible for me to recall all the endurance walk events in which I took part. Despite the singular peculiarities, individual challenges, and the rigour associated with each event, there were so many that I do not remember them all. However, there are some that I will always remember. One of them was a walk around the clock staged at the Stadium in Hong Kong. It was organised on behalf of charity to include and benefit all the different nationalities residing in the area. As I reflect, it is still remembered as one of my most strenuous walks ever undertaken. The effort was devised to be a way by which the British troops in the area could lead the way in making a charitable contribution to all the people of Hong Kong.

As with my other walks, there were set rules. All the participants were not expected to walk for twenty-four hours. Some of the participants were to compete as individuals while others competed in groups, or as teams. When the competitors operated as a group, at least one person was expected to complete the whole walk. Everyone was required to walk as fast as he or she could throughout the event. Two of the competitors were the stars of the event. Each was a champion in his own right. One man was black, the other white. Both men had to complete the entire walk and both were trying to break the 120-mile record for a twenty-four-hour walk. At the time, the black man, John Brooks, held the record for the most miles walked in seventy-five hours of continuous walking. It stood at a total of 305 miles. The other man, Roy Bailey, was champion for the twenty-five mile run and for the heel-to-toe two-mile walk. In the Hong Kong race, I was doing more than a walk for charity. I was also challenging myself to an unusual performance. During the preparation, I trained daily for seven or eight hours because I wanted to do well in the event.

Rain started to pour on the walkers about 10 PM, on the Saturday, with the race set to finish at 10 AM the following day. The weather kept being both rainy and windy, but the walkers kept on. Despite the unpleasant weather condition, I recall saying to the reporters that I loved the fact that it was raining, since I hated walking in the heat. Meanwhile, everyone was aware that by Sunday afternoon someone would be crowned the champion walker.

When the walk started, the interest was at a very high level; all the competitors were excited. There were uniformed bodies such as youth clubs and youths who were confined to wheel chairs. They participated in the race as teams. The event was organised to be both a fun day and as an activity to raise money for the charity chest of the community. As a lead-up to the big walk event, there were opportunities to participate in some preliminary activities. On January 15, 1978, for example, some 30,000 walkers took part in a walk which the *South China Morning Post* captioned as "Happy Feet Walk for a Million." Soon, as never before, the people in Hong Kong took notice of our fund raising activity and became excited, as they began to focus on our up and coming endurance walk as a very special event. It had been a long time since the whole society in Hong Kong paid so much attention to anything done on their island by the British military. Generally, they saw themselves as colonised and the British military as an invading force.

Prior to my being moved to the Hong Kong area, Police Inspector Bailey starred as the fit-man and athletic champion in Hong Kong. However, when I was sent to Hong Kong, that situation was about to change. In the special Hong Kong race, I came up against Inspector Bailey and another policeman, Adrian Norman, from the Kowloon City Police Station. Both were expected to do well in the competition. However, Norman dropped out early. Bailey and I were left with each other, one-on-one; and both of us could not win. The walk started at 10 AM on the Saturday. By midnight it became evident that I was virtually on my own, but Bailey was quite relaxed too and remained very much in the competition. We both stopped for short spells, to eat, drink, and to talk with relatives. The rest of the competitors consisted of some eleven other teams.

From time to time, there were indications by the onlookers that some persons were having problems with sprained ankles, as the rain kept pouring. However, I remained on the course walking smoothly, and felt very strong. My intention was that not even the poor weather would make me finish under the twenty-four hours set for the event. Eventually, it started to appear that both the raindrops and the breeze invigorated me. I was also interested in the prospect of breaking the twenty-four-hour walk record of 133 miles. Bailey withdrew at midnight, but the weather condition prevented me from breaking the record. However, I went on to complete 109 miles in the twenty-four hours, walking around the stadium 422 times. The winning team was from the English land force and the second place team was that representing the Huang Da Xian Social Services. Two female teams also finished the race.

Despite the inclement weather, the event proved to be a very successful effort covered by some twenty-seven newspapers, plus television and radio stations. All the participants appeared to have enjoyed themselves. On May 17, 1978, the company commander, Lieutenant Colonel John Hambly, presented the community chest director Mr. Graham Henderson with a cheque worth 45,999.60 Hong Kong dollars. I donated the other 40 cents bringing the amount to 46,000. 00 Hong Kong dollars. After my unit gave the cheque, it also received something in return. We were presented the Wilkinson's Sword of Peace, an award that usually went to infantry units. It was awarded to our unit for all the community service we undertook and accomplished in Hong

Kong. We reached out into the schools and community and built important bridges, as we interacted with the people of Hong Kong. Prior to our staging the endurance walk event, the local people doubted that it could happen because of the intense heat. However, the walk took place and turned out to be a major success. It remains among my most challenging and also my most memorable walking events.

Endurance walking was one of the interests and accomplishments that I came to be associated with during my service in the British military. It was one of the interests in my life that developed from my day-to-day involvement with the army. The soldier's life of discipline, austerity, and competiveness provided me the martial experiences, made me a participant, a competitor, a winner, and a charitable giver as an endurance walker. Eventually, I understood how I could couple endurance walking with charitable giving and self development. For me, psychologically and physically, the sport became much more than just placing severe stress on the body. The skill of endurance walking contributed to my development of independence, my strong will, and my deep commitment to making a difference in the lives of those broken helpless others, when I can. Also, it enhanced my ability to think deeply. It improved and built my competitive-ness.; And it connected me to the poor and the powerless.

At times, endurance walking also brought me much personal satisfaction. While it worked to increase my competiveness it taught me persistence at tasks, led to the setting of new records, and the winning of trophies in important competitions. Over time, endurance walking became a part of my life's experience which I will never forget. There were also the many persons of comparable fitness and tenacity against whom I competed. Some of us developed long-term friendships despite our severe, aggressive competitions. From 1974 to the 1980s, competitive walking became very much a part of my personal life, shaping a peculiar culture and experience. Maybe there are persons who will see it as being insane for someone to cover such gruelling distances again and again. However, my response to such thinking is simple. There was always the challenge to help persons less fortunate than myself. Often there were those who could not walk or run, due to no fault of their own. Endurance walking was a different, but interesting way of raising money to help such persons. Another benefit I realised from walking was the personal satisfaction and the maintenance of good health which I experienced and loved. Other persons also appeared to value the challenge and the other benefits that came to their lives from endurance walking. For example, there was one event in which I participated during 1975. About one hundred and fifty other persons took part in the activity. They must have found the experience useful and gratifying. Years later in Hong Kong, it was unusual, but interesting, that the whole community came together and focused, with such interest on an endurance walking competition, for many months. As with any other demanding sport activity, in endurance walking, one has to be prepared to face the challenges of physical and mental hardships during the preparation and during the competitions. Another powerful force that kept me going on and on, during my endurance-walk competitions, was a strong determination to succeed at whatever I did, even when it challenged my physical and mental wellbeing to the extent that endurance walking did. .

Probably, endurance walking came to interest me when I looked around for something different to pursue as an interest in my life because I was in the military and exposed to severe physical challenges. Such a life was in line with walking for many miles at a time, to the point of insanity. If I had the opportunity to live my life over again, I would want to start endurance walking at an earlier point in my life. Today, it is impossible for me to recall all the endurance walking events in which I was involved. However, I would be remiss if I ever forget the one at Aintree that started it all—it started my walking career. The walk from Buckingham Palace to Liverpool Town Hall deserves mention, for we were greeted by the Mayor at the Town Hall and served coffee, then went back to Aintree to see the annual walk started, for that year. My walk from Birkenhead to Plymouth was also a memorable event. In 1976, as a result of my friendship with Corporal Russ Phillips of the Canadian forces, I travelled to Canada and participated in a charity walk there. The walks where I won trophies or set new records were also memorable to me. I still recall both the challenges and the satisfaction I experienced from such endeavours. The memories I continue to hold from such walking experiences are many and varied. Some are still very vibrant and real. At times, when I reflect on specific events, I still seem to feel the physical pain to my body, from that long, long past. For example, that walk in Brunei to help the Gurkhas Welfare Fund went for 30 miles and there were twenty walkers. Because of the great heat, it took longer than expected. For the first time, I was beaten into second place by a local walker. However, we did raise a good sum of money for the cause.

There was also a painful experience that came to overwhelm and stun me. It reached back to the height of my walking days. After my many years of walking, working, and sharing with charity, something I discovered made me very disillusioned and sad. It was a painful experience when I learned that some of the persons who administered the charities were not always honest and ethical, as they handled and managed the money we donated to the charities. Quite often the funds were spent foolishly and selfishly by the administrators. Much of it did not get down to the lower levels of the organisations to help the poor and powerless persons who really stood in need. Seemingly, my strenuous efforts to earn that cash for charity often did not achieve what it was meant to do, since it was diverted and used for other purposes. Despite my disappointment, I did not stop giving to charity. I simply changed to charities such as Save the Children Fund, and to other charities that I knew managed the donations in an ethical and transparent manner.

I will always remember that initially, the experience of becoming a soldier was a strange, frightening challenge for me. However, I learned to enjoy being a British soldier. Today, I am still amazed at how soldiering remade and changed my life. Despite my pleasant experiences from being a soldier, in this life, time is not on one's life forever. Consequently, nothing, not even my soldiering experiences, could last forever. On March 24th, 1984, after twenty-six years of growing, changing, and living a soldier's life, I gritted my teeth, turned my back, and said goodbye to soldiering. It was a dramatic interruption to the patterning of my life, but I could not soldier forever.

With the support of my wife and children, I stepped away from what I did for twenty-six years and made a move to the world of business. Just like when I began soldiering, business was something new for me. However, I had been exposed to management experiences as a soldier. My success in soldiering led me to conclude that a person's ignorance about what an experience really is, should not be the best means by which to judge how becoming immersed in that experience can impact one's life. Rather, when that experience is tried, one may become intrigued at how his or her life can grow and change, as a result of the new experience. The impact of that new exposure can even come to overwhelm one's life. That was a profound lesson I learned after becoming a British soldier. Now, I was prepared to observe what other lessons I could learn about life, and how I could grow from taking a plunge of faith into business.

My Early Walking Experience-John White Shoes
with son Andrew looking on (1975)

My Early Walking Experience- Advertising Shoes

Welcome Cuthridge Field, Canada

Phillips and Brooks before their Canadian Walk

A Person Of The Year 1975

Brooks and Challengers-Ready to walk a marathon for charity

The
NSPCC
TROPHY

I WAS THE PROUD OWNER
OF THIS TROPHY FOR ONE
YEAR IT STAND ABOUT
2 FEET TALL DURING THE
YEAR SECURITY WAS A PROBLEM

With The NSPCC Trophy 2

The British European Commonwealth Endurance Walking Record, 1971

The Trophy for the World record Endurance Walking 1975

Presented with trophy for world record, 1975 - 289 mile non-stop

Greetings from

the

British, European & Commonwealth Record Holder

for Endurance Walking

24 - 29 May 1974	Distance 290 miles
29 June - 4 July 1974	Distance 291.75 miles

My Calling Card Campaigning Card

Cold beats record bid

JOHN BROOKS, a 39-year-old staff sergeant with the Royal Army Ordnance Corps at Bicester, just failed today in his attempt to set a new world walking record.

He gave up in the NSPCC marathon walk at Aintree racecourse, Liverpool, after 290 miles — 12 miles short of his target. He had walked non-stop since Friday night, except for occasional breaks.

Brooks (right) said later: "The cold beat me — the Aintree circuit is very open and very bleak."

One of his Army pacers said Brooks was still in good physical condition when he gave up.

"He had only one small blister on his foot. His failure was a mental thing, rather than physical. It was so cold and desolate out there — he just couldn't keep going," he said.

One consolation for Brooks — who was helped during the race by his wife, three children and two teams of soldiers from Bicester —

was that he broke the British and Commonwealth walking record of 256 miles.

After giving up at 5.45 a.m. today, he was taken to Walton Hospital, Liverpool, for a check-up and rest.

He averaged about 25 minutes for each 1.64 mile lap of the circuit. Just before he stopped, he was still lapping in 34 minutes — faster than the speed at which some competitors had started.

Mr Dick Crawshaw, MP for Toxteth, Liverpool, dropped out after setting a new record of 231 miles for non-stop walking.

Hot footing it to a world record

By DENNIS PHILLIPS

John Brooks set out on a hot, muggy morning yesterday for a walk around Hongkong Stadium — 422 times around to be exact.

That's how far he will have to go to set a new world record for the 24-hour walk. Staff Sergeant Brooks already holds the world endurance record of going 305 miles in a 75-hour walk, set in 1975.

But apart from the new record, Sgt Brooks also hopes to raise $30,000 for the Community Chest, helped along by two policemen and 10 teams.

The first part of the "Walk Around the Clock" went very smoothly, but the hot, humid weather could take its toll later.

Dehydration is one of the big problems faced by endurance athletes, according to observers.

Mrs Audrey Brooks had a bag full of glucose drinks, honey and fruit to help her husband along on his record-breaking attempt.

"I add a pinch of salt to the glucose drinks, as he doesn't like salt tablets," Mrs Brooks said. "He likes the occasional chicken leg, and lots of fruit, which he can eat on the way around. And in the morning he'll have porridge."

Sgt Brooks, from Anguilla, West Indies, became interested in walking when posted to Germany, where competitive walks and runs are held almost every weekend. In 1976 he was awarded the British Empire Medal for his charity fund-raising efforts.

"I think this 24-hour walk is more gruelling than his record (305 mile) walk," said Mrs Brooks, as her husband heel-and-toed past.

"Then he could set his own pace, but now he's rushing to beat the clock."

Sgt Brooks started in the company of two policemen, Roy Bailey of the Police Training School and Adrian Norman, who decided to give it a go when his Kowloon City Police Station team already had the full complement of six members.

The three were to try for the full 24 hours. However, Mr Norman fell a victim to the heat and dropped out in the afternoon.

(Cont'd on Page 6, Col 7)

Elder daughter Jackie helps Staff Sgt Brooks on his record-breaking attempt with thirst-quenching fruit juice — By Sunny Lee.

My Walking Years

All wound up for a round the clock walk

STAFF Sgt. John Brooks's boots sure are made for walking. . .

He's already walked nearly 300 miles to become the British, European and Commonwealth champion endurance walker. And next month he plans to clock up another 140 miles or so—this time inside 24 hours.

Staff Sgt. Brooks (right), a 39-year-old West Indian, hopes to set a new 24-hour non-stop world record at Aldershot Military Stadium on May 10 and 11. The current record is 133 miles.

Several other top walkers have been invited to compete against Staff Sgt. Brooks in the sponsored walk, being held in aid of the Army Benevolent Fund. They include the world record endurance holder Mr. Edward Jugo (he walked 304 miles), the MP for Toxeter, Liverpool, Col. Dick Crawshaw, and Bristol's "walking grandma," Mrs. Dorothy Jannone (63).

BLISTERS

Staff Sgt. Brooks, of the Royal Army Ordnance Corps, Blackdown training centre, Deepcut, trains for about two hours every night and thinks nothing of popping down the road to Slough or Basingstoke—on foot. He averages between five and seven miles an hour in training, and about four to five when competing.

A father of three, he has an iron will and said "Walking is a matter of forgetting about pain and tiredness. I get blisters, sure I get them, just like everyone else, but I just don't think about them.

"The pain barrier comes at about the 50 mile mark. Once you've passed that, you keep going because your determination takes over from your legs."

He says he makes up nursery rhymes and stories to keep his mind alert as he walks. Ideas for these come from advertising signs or notices he passes.

CROWD

"If there were anyone walking beside me, I'd have written about four or five books full by now," he laughed.

The walk's organiser, Staff Sgt. Chris Forbes-Ritte, hopes a large crowd will watch the walk.

He said, "We don't expect them to stay the whole 24 hours, but we're hoping people will come in for say 20 minutes, then go away, and come back again later."

APRIL 75

Former Bicester soldier takes world walking title

A former Bicester soldier, Staff Sgt John Brooks, has his name in the Guinness Book of Records — once again.

A long distance walker, John Brooks got his name in this celebrated book of records last year when he took the British and Commonwealth non-stop walking title by covering a distance of 290 miles at the Aintree motor-racing circuit. The previous record was 256.8 miles.

As if this distance was not enough, Staff Sgt Brooks has now taken the world title by covering a distance of 305.44 miles,

also at Aintree, to beat the previous record of 304 miles.

This staggering distance was covered in 75 hours and during the event he was sponsored to raise money for the National Society for the Prevention of Cruelty to Children.

Last year when Staff Sgt Brooks attempted the world non-stop walking title he retired because of the cold after covering a distance of 109 miles.

At the time he was stationed at 16 Battalion RAOC, Bicester Garrison. Recently he was transferred to Camberley in Surrey.

BICESTER ADVERTISER
17 SEPT 75

World walking Title

FAREWELL WAVE
. . . Russ Phillips

BROOKS KEEPS WALKING
. . . to reach 350 miles
— Times-Herald Photos

Two Walking Rivals Title

My Walking Years

Success though no record

STAFF Sergeant John Brooks failed yesterday morning in his attempt to walk his way into the record books by covering more than 133 miles in 24 hours.

In the end it was just too much, but it would be wrong to say that he failed. More important his children thought he was just great and they amply rewarded him (above).

After slogging through day and night, heat and humidity, blisters and fatigue, he clocked up 101 miles and 1467 yards — how can you call that failure?

In fact, nobody contributed more than John Brooks to the success of Walk Around The Clock. He drew a large crowd of well-wishers, press and television to the Hongkong Stadium.

Walk Around The Clock was staged to raise money for the Community Chest.

H K

I DID THE WALKING AND AS YOU
WILL SEE FROM THE ABOVE PAPER
CUTTING, BUT NOT WITHOUT THE SUP-
PORT OF THE CHLDREN, ON A TRACK
WAS EASY FOR AUDREY # HAVING
THE SMALL CHILDRED IT WAS
LIKE HELL FOR HER HAVING TO
DRIVE TWO MILES DOWN THE ROAD
PARK AND WAIT FOR ME TO REACH
THAT AREA DRINK FOOD CHANGE
SOCKS AND OFF SHE WENT AGAINT
WEATHER IT BE DAY OR NIGHT
THE CHILDREN SLEEPT IN THE CAR.

My Walking Years

97

Chapter Eight

From Soldiering to Business

The confidence and independence that I developed in the military and from my experiences with endurance walking were factors influencing my next move beyond the military. They suggested to me that I required an independent life after my soldiering career was over. Consequently, I had no intention to work for anyone after I left the armed forces. Even before my stint with the military was over, I started to think about what I could do after the army. Despite my maturity and independence, I was not quite certain what I wanted to do with my life when I separated from the military. For month after month, I browsed through the national papers. I was hoping that something interesting would catch my eye. One day, I saw an advertisement about how to start your own small business. Following that, I made contact with the advertiser. On receiving the needed information, I reviewed it carefully, then began to plan the start of my own business. At first I thought about becoming a private detective, since I had experiences as a regimental police officer in the army. While I was still thinking about becoming a private detective, another idea for independent entrepreneurship came to my mind.

My second idea was to focus on selling textiles and electronics, including jeans, sweatshirts, moccasins, and also electrical goods. Such an approach to my business setup was particularly attractive because it would not require major capital outlay, provided I kept the initial setup of the business small. Meanwhile, after some investigation, I became aware that finding wholesalers for the merchandise that interested me would not be a real problem. Accordingly, I began my experience in business selling material, which I knew would go quickly. After a short time in business, the process became hard work and more demanding than I first thought it could be. Initially, I still had a full-time job with the army, travelled frequently, and therefore could only operate the business on a part-time basis. The transportation used for my business was also very unreliable. Unfortunately, even though I was aware of that problem, I was not in a financial position to change it. For example, I needed to travel to Wolverhampton, to High Wycombe, Birmingham and elsewhere to purchase merchandise and meet my clientele. However, doing such travel at evenings and during the winter months, using unreliable transportation was not very attractive to me. I became concerned about handling frequent vehicular breakdown. Dealing with such matters during long distance travel affected the business, my personal stress level, and my satisfaction.

Despite the drawbacks that threatened to undermine and limit the success of my business endeavour, I remained a determined entrepreneur intent on making my enterprise a success. At that time, the popular fashion included jeans and sweatshirts, for both ladies and men. They were in high demand and sold quickly. My strategy was to concentrate on the quick sellers while at the same time moving to expand into other areas. Quite often, my wife who worked as a full-time nurse had to give up her weekends to assist with the pricing process. She did not really like the idea of giving up her Saturdays and Sundays off to tag merchandise. The children also pitched in and help where possible.

However, we were still uncertain about the viability of the textile business and our chances of success. It was as we debated our next move, and what would be a venture more amenable to both of us, that Audrey proposed the idea of our opening and operating a nursing home. However, I did not agree initially. Running a nursing home was a totally new area of involvement for me. My knowledge about managing a nursing home was extremely limited and somewhat threatening to me. I realised that my wife would have to take the lead and I would have to trust her judgment and wisdom in dealing with the new venture. We were agreeing to enter a business that was highly regulated, needed heavy financial outlay, and was a sector of business dominated by whites. One redeeming factor was that my wife and I were quite competent in our individual fields; she a nurse and I a general administrator. A second factor was also critical to our venture's success. I had a very good credit rating at the bank where I did business for a number of years.

We sat as a family, my wife, my children, and I, and we shared lengthy discussions. As best we could, we used all the information available and reviewed the business possibilities. It was finally agreed that the nursing home idea, suggested by Audrey, was our best business prospect. Consequently, we agreed to make a meaningful investment in that direction, while opting out of the other things with which we were involved. Soon after, we started to look around for a building with the location and capacity to meet our requirements for a nursing home. As fate would have it, we discovered that there was a large, run-down and dilapidated property in our vicinity. It was up for auction by the local authorities. Despite fierce competition from other interests, my bid for the property was successful. Once we were certain of a building, we then approached a bank to get the necessary financing. Care was taken to ensure that proper plans and financial projections for the project were in place to share and discuss with the bankers. The bank saw our proposals as being worthwhile and sensible. Without too much hesitation, the financing for our nursing home project was approved. We agreed on the name, BROOKLANDS NURSING HOME, and continued our planning to start the business.

There were numerous drawbacks associated with the building and getting it ready for the purpose we had in mind. One of our first problems was that we had to deal with two feet of water in the cellar. Since the water was sitting there for a long time, it caused extensive dampness in the woodwork and throughout the building. Another problem was that vines were growing through the broken windows, into the doors, and in the brickwork. When we entered the building at first, we were surrounded by an eerie atmosphere and very creepy, ghostly feelings. The picture inside the building was one of dreariness and a forgotten loneliness. Nothing about the building was welcoming. We looked at one another and each of us mused over the same question quietly, "Where do we start?"

A large, empty water tank sat in the cellar. Part of one wall had to be removed and the tank hauled up the stairs of the cellar in order to get rid of it from the building. Then, we used buckets to get rid of the water sitting on the floor. After that task was completed, we started to sense that we were getting some place with our effort to transform the building. As part of our reclaiming programme, the roof had to be stripped and retiled in order to protect the building from the harsh, inclement weather. Other extensive renovations had to be done to upgrade the building and make it a welcoming place to our clientele. It was a blessing that I had experience with building because we had limited cash and needed to do all we could to cut cost. I did quite a bit of the work, except that having to do with electricity, gas, plumbing, and central heating. That type of work required expertise, which I knew little about. It was assigned to persons who were experts in these areas. Eventually, with determined effort and a high level of perseverance, after some time, the building was renovated and started to take shape as a place that could accommodate patients as a nursing home. Even as we completed the repairs, it was discovered that there were other problems associated with the project that had to be addressed. For example, we needed the correct equipment to ensure that all the stipulations set for such a building were met. There were also special rules to meet and legal requirements which had to be carefully adhered to and met. We paid careful attention to meeting all the set requirements for a nursing home. Eventually, all the perceived and the anticipated problems were overcome. Some of these were great challenges, however, we persevered. In time, we managed to restore the waterlogged, dilapidated building we took over to at least some of its former glory.

Notwithstanding our creative efforts, there was no easy route to getting the building registered as a nursing home. The bureaucracy we encountered was not very welcoming or accommodating. Here again, as with my endurance walking, my courage, my will, and my iron determination kept me pushing at the officials. I would not give up. It was possible that behind some of the hesitation we observed among the officials was related to the fact that my family was the first black proprietors owning and managing a nursing home in the Banbury area. Admittedly, I, too, was surprised and expectant about the enterprise on which we were embarking. But my family agreed on the venture and we were determined to see it through.

With the structural and regulation problems behind us, we moved to open our new nursing home business on June 1, 1984. We were advised that our business was the fifteenth nursing home registered in that area of Oxfordshire at the time. Meanwhile, we had become so committed to meeting all the requirements and to be ready for our grand opening that we overlooked the necessity to advertise we were about to open the facility. However, we did open as planned. When the guests arrived for the opening, we discovered that someone had overlooked the delivery of the cooker. Also, the electricity could not be used because of problems with the grounding wires. As a result, the electricity inspector refused to give the necessary permission for operation until the correct earth wires had been fitted. It was about six o'clock that evening before we could really open our doors and start operating as a nursing home. Within days of our official opening, we accepted our first patient. Our capacity at opening was nineteen beds. In a short time, the demand for beds in nursing homes became so critical that by August, all nineteen in our facility were full. Soon, we started to be advertised word of mouth, person to person, throughout the area. Our facility kept receiving constant demand for new bookings. However, we could not fulfill all the demands because of our limited bed capacity. Accordingly, not long after, we made plans to expand the facility by six single rooms. These were well received by our clientele and turned out to be preferred over shared accommodation.

By 1987, three years after our opening, we began to realise the goals that were set for our business. The facility had stabilised and was performing in a very reliable, efficient, and productive manner. Because of our growing success, including the level of profitability, we also started to consider the possibility for further expansion to our business. A number of buildings were suggested to us as possibilities. However, contractors had already earmarked some for sheltered housing and others for apartment blocks. After a time, one of the other nursing homes nearby was placed on the market. Since we understood the growth potential of such a business, we purchased the other nursing home. Our aim was to expand in the area of about thirty-two bedrooms. Three years into the business, we were much better prepared to deal with emerging issues and to resolve management problems, while we kept our business functioning efficiently. By the late 1980s, early 1990s, the nursing home business was beginning to appear quite easy to set up and manage, as compared with what we had to deal with when we started the business in 1984. Soon both establishments were running smoothly and our staff grew to seventy workers.

To some persons, the setup and maintenance of a nursing home in Britain during the 1980s might have appeared easy. Such a conclusion was far from the truth. Functioning fairly and honestly in the nursing home business is never easy. We were always challenged to work hard and do our best. We kept high standards and there was always the aim to please our clientele. During our operation, the patients ranged in age from 55 to 103 years old. Just as I had worked hard at soldiering and endurance walking, I kept working hard at maintaining and managing my nursing home business successfully. There were times when I had no alternative but to work late into the nights to complete assignments and meet deadlines. What my business venture became in just under twenty years, could never have been attained without a measure of vision, careful organisation, hard work, and a commitment to success. Meanwhile, we were constantly under the microscope being monitored by the nursing home authorities. The fire brigade checked us regularly, so too did the catering officers, the hygiene officers, and the pharmacy regulators. We were made aware of the regulations before our business started, and we worked to stay in line. Usually, the inspections were very stressful. In some cases, the inspections included regulations on paper that had no bearing on what took place inside the nursing home. Notwithstanding, I found my working in the nursing home business to be enjoyable and very rewarding. The compliments from the families and persons served were always received with great appreciation. Generally, the nurses and the other persons who worked with us were wonderful and conscientious people. One nurse that comes to mind readily is Sister Eilish Houlihan. She worked at the nursing home faithfully from 1984 until she retired. We held a special ceremony, covered by the local newspaper, to say goodbye to Sister Houlihan as she retired. Everyone at the nursing home continues to remember her as "a smashing sister." Over time, I also became aware that the business was placing me in line to reap some positive social and political benefits.

Despite our commitment to the nursing home business, the time came when we opted to get out and walk away from it. Throughout the years, we felt under pressure from the monitoring groups. At one time, I was asked to close one of the floors, so that my business capacity would decrease by one third. The frustration and harassment reminded me of my military days when confidential reports were written indicating that I was a brilliant soldier, however, before the report ended there was a demeaning "BUT." Each year, the monitoring by the authorities became more severe. My business was fully integrated, but at times I wondered whether race was not a major factor colouring the thoroughness and severity of the inspections. We also learned that other nursing home businesses in the area, run by white management, did not experience the same level of harassment. The medical profession and the persons we served were both satisfied with our performance.

However, with an aging British population, there were growing possibilities and the competition in the nursing home business was blossoming. As a niche for investment, the nursing home business was becoming increasingly attractive to new entrepreneurs. By 2003, my family had been in the nursing home business for nineteen years. During that time, we served over 2,000 residents in need of care. Their ages ranged from 55 to

over 100 years. I am still very proud about the direction in which my wife nudged our family business and how the experiment turned out. Our nursing home was a business designed to touch lives and bring empathy to the process of dealing with aging persons, some pushed aside from the centre of life's stage, and often just waiting to die. However, making a profit was important, so there was always the challenge to keep the business vibrant, welcoming, and certainly profitable. There were standards to meet, bills to pay, and demands from continuous change were always present. Meanwhile, since economic success and social progress have caused the extended family patterning to decline, while life expectancy is expanding, there is growing demand for the services of nursing homes and rehabilitation centres. We did take all these factors and circumstances into account as we managed our business. Notwithstanding, after nineteen years in the business, my family and I made the decision to sell it and get out. There were monetary attractions; we also enjoyed helping stressed, broken, and lonely people. But the demands of the business and the scrutiny from the authorities were becoming too overwhelming. By 2003, the nursing home business had become too cumbersome and demanding an enterprise for our liking and comfort. It was no longer an easy venture to manage, or one that brought us satisfaction like before. We invested almost twenty years of our lives in the business. However, leaving our nursing home facility was something we made up our minds to do, as a family. Once we reached that decision, we were determined to live with it as a family agreement. So we sold out and moved on.

June 30, 2003 will remain an important time in my forever memory. That was when we walked away from our once treasured nursing home business. It is an event I relive constantly, and about which I still ask the question, "Did I do the right thing?" On that memorable day my family and I walked away from the nursing home business, which we created and managed for many years. I recall that at the closing ceremony I said, "Today, the 30th June 2003, we celebrate the end of nineteen years of hard work and ask you all to join with us in celebrating the end of this era." Present at the final Brookland Nursing Home celebration were the Mayor of Banbury, the area's parliamentary representative, and some other friends. Audrey and I liked what we were doing, but we were getting older and were beginning to feel the difference in our bodies. The stresses and strains associated with the business had become unbearable. Accordingly, we decided the time was right for us to retire, and this time stay retired. It occurred to me, too, that the time had come when I should wake up late in the morning, draw the curtains, and see the sun shining through, even when the weather is cloudy.

However, despite the dreams for my life of retirement, I could not just walk away from involvement in my community. I had been a soldier, businessman, and a fundraiser for charities. It was not within me to simply withdraw myself from my community. There had to be something else in the society to challenge and inspire my life. Could it be that I had the guts and the desire to become a politician—something that always nudged my thinking? Or, was I prepared to simply slip away into oblivion; just disappear from the centre of the action? These were questions that I began to ask myself.

The answers came very soon. I could not stay retired. Time had made me too much a part of the community of Banbury. It was difficult for me to just fade away quietly. Since I was very much alive and in good health, there were other dreams to follow and some mountains I had not yet climbed. Maybe I could find it within myself to go around again. Even before I left the nursing home business, I started to feel an urge towards the political life. Having served as a soldier, then having done so much for charities over the years, plus my later involvement with running a nursing home in the city of Banbury, all served to get me some political capital, which I could use at some time in the future. I knew about that possibility, because even while I was involved with the nursing home business, there were those who enticed me towards politics.

Brooklands no. 1 opening day June 1, 1984

Brooklands no. 2 being opened 1985

Brooks with Nursing Home Staff Brookland 2003

Brooklands Nursing Home no. 1

Brooklands Nursing Home no. 2

■ CHEERS: Staff at Brooklands Nursing Home raised their glasses on Wednesday to wish Sister Eilish Houlihan a happy retirement.

A Retirement From Brooklands

Chapter Nine

Councillor, Magistrate, Mayor

Once I was through with the military, I did not return to Slough. Rather, I chose to live in Banbury, a small city some 160 miles from Slough. When I lived at Slough, I was new to England and settled at a place which was chosen for me. Further, when I vacated the military in 1984, I was a much more independent and confident person, as compared to when I landed in England back in 1955, and just trying to find my way. Along with changing my place of abode on leaving the army, I also started to look for new directions into which I could thrust my life and find meaning. Entrepreneurship and business ownership came readily to mind because after twenty-six years in the military, I had learned a great deal of independence, and about organisational management. In time, politics started to become increasingly attractive to me. There was still time for me to continue reaching out towards new challenges for my life. I could try out at other activities, despite the fact that the logistics with which I had become accustomed, in the military, were missing. Accordingly, I moved in the direction of politics as early as 1985, one year after being out of the military. The next year, in 1986, and for a number of years, I served as a magistrate in the Banbury area. Then in 2005, I had the most joyous surprise of my life. That was the year when I achieved the honour of being appointed Mayor of Banbury, the city where I had lived, set up business, and involved myself for just over twenty years.

My first venture in Banbury was into business, not politics; however, I made the time and continued to work with charities. The nature of my initial business, as a textile salesman, made it time consuming, but I found the time to continue my association with charitable organisations. As fate had it, over time, my business ventures and my association with a number of charities in the area did help me to build a useful stock of political capital. Accordingly, persons who paid attention to political possibilities started to recognise my worth and soon began to entice me towards that direction. Since I did not have much to lose, I accepted the challenge and started my journey into politics by joining the local branch of the Conservative Party at Banbury in 1985. At that time I had no particular political dream in mind. I was simply excited by the idea of becoming a part of the political process in Britain. One year later, I was approached by the party leaders and asked to become a candidate in the local elections for the Cherwell District Council, in Neithrop Ward, at Bretch Hill. It was a Labour Party stronghold and my party did not expect me to do well. Politically, I was the sacrificial lamb for the Conservative Party.

While I accepted the challenge to run a campaign in an area I knew little about, I was very aware that both the Conservative Party and the Labour Party had a strategy of placing their best effort behind their safe seats. For the Conservative Party, mine was not one. However, I did not support the idea of safe and unsafe seats. What I thought at the time, and still do, is that each voter should be given an opportunity to share his or her opinion. With that thinking behind my approach to politics, I set out with a particular plan in mind. My strategy was to canvass every home, on ever street in the Neithrop Ward. As I campaigned, I shared as many of my leaflets as I could with the populace. I also took the time and spoke with as many persons as would listen to me. . At no time during my initial effort was I accompanied by any member of the Conservative Party, since the area had been labeled a Labour stronghold and a sure Labour Party seat. It was reasoned that with me being in the race, the Conservatives could argue that they were represented in the district.

The campaign experience was interesting and very rewarding for me. Since I was campaigning on my own, there were opportunities for me to sit and chat one and one with residents in the area. Many shared their problems with me and I was able to bring about some change in certain situations. Some of the problems I encountered were clearly related to political neglect and the powerlessness of the people in the area. There were houses with windows boarded up, or with ugly broken glass windows. Many lorries were illegally parked, while their official parking areas were left empty. All around the area I saw signs of neglect, so I made these some of my major talking points, as I canvassed the area. It did not matter to me whether it was mainly a Conservative or Labour constituency. Many persons living in the area had been neglected over time, and that had to change.

After my frequent visits and exchanges with the electorate, I started to experience a sense of growing confidence and increased recognition in the area. Accordingly, I invited my local member of Parliament to visit and canvass the constituency with me. Despite our having conflicting political views, the Parliamentarian was allowed to see and hear the concerns of the people there. At the same time, I kept my argument going that everybody should be treated humanely; their politics should not be a limiting factor to their community, its living conditions, or to its development. My views were accepted as useful and some of my concerns started to receive action. Since that time, there have been signs of growing change and progress in that community.

As could be expected, not everyone I met in the area liked the idea that I was a West Indian championing the cause of the Conservative Party. There were comments such as, "You are black, you should be supporting the Labour Party"; "What do you think the Conservative Party will ever do for you?"; "Do you expect to be treated fairly by that party?" However, such comments did not deter me. I continued to do what I felt was best for the area, and what would allow me a respectable finish on election day. Members of my family were my main support during the campaign. On election day, the party sent me a temporary assistant. Soon after the election process started, he was called and sent to another location before the voting was over. Despite my neglect by the party, I kept a vibrant campaign going right up to the election day. I lost that election, my first try as a political candidate, by fifty votes. I did much better than anyone expected. However, the experience was disheartening for me. In retrospect, I felt that I was put out to the wolves and left there—alone. While I remained with the Conservative Party, I took no active part in party events for a long time. All I did was to give limited assistance in some of the later local elections. One positive fall-out from my political involvement was that my nursing home business prospered. Many new elderly clients started to enter the nursing home.

Despite the disillusionment I experienced after my first venture into politics, my enticement towards politics did not go away. Quietly I started to edge towards politics again in 1996. Finally, after my first try fifteen years before, I was chosen by my party to try again in the year 2000. When approached by the Conservative Party to be a candidate in the Calthrope Ward, I did not hesitate. I accepted the challenge to become a councillor and won the election in May, 2000. Later in 2002, the first town council was organised. None of the councillors had prior training. We were all novices to the demands ahead. There was a comprehensive code of conduct and guide for good practice. Since I was an ex-soldier, neither the code of conduct nor the guide for good practice bothered me. I recalled my years in the army where we treated one another with respect; we respected the law and we were able to observe the impartiality of our superiors. It was there that I learned to value confidentiality and above all to act with honesty. The requirements for the councillors refreshed my military training and helped my preparation for the role I came to play in the town council.

While I served as a member of the council, I found the work interesting. We worked in committees where decisions were really made in the best interest of the town's citizens. I also became involved in various community-building activities. There were times when I represented the town council at meetings of bodies such as the Old People's Club, Cherwell Planning Partnership 2016, served as a director for Carers West Oxfordshire, and also assisted with the Citizens Advice Bureau. For me, that type of community involvement was very meaningful and rewarding. I was delighted and proud to be involved with my community in such a manner. For a number of years, I worked with both the Calthorpe Ward and the Banbury Town Council. Every opportunity to participate in decision making for these communities was considered a unique and exceptional opportunity to impact lives and ensure further development in the area. The town council was supported by an administration staff and managed by a town clerk, who was responsible for running the office and its activities.

Being a town councillor is a voluntary, unpaid assignment. Candidates have to be prepared to accept the responsibility for attending committee meetings and giving general support within the council. There were three main functions for the resources committee that dealt with town planning and financial matters. The general services committee dealt with the welfare and upkeep of the town. There was a planning committee, which had the task of monitoring planning applications. Each councillor had the opportunity to choose and work with one of the committees. The bonus value to serving as a councillor is that it allows a person experience with community responsibility and exposure to building community respect. It also places one in line to become Mayor of the town. The individual also gains social status as he or she is placed in the limelight, so that the society can be served in various other capacities.

Unlike other persons, I did not apply to become a magistrate in Banbury. Seemingly, I was selected out and nominated by the community. The first time I knew about my nomination was when I received a call inviting me for an interview on a particular date. The challenge of being a magistrate made me nervous, since I had no legal background. However, I responded to the call and went for the interview. Three senior chairmen magistrates and a court clerk conducted the interview. The questions were largely about my political beliefs. That session was followed by questions on a paper, which could be completed in twenty minutes. In June 1989, thirty-seven other individuals, along with myself, were sworn in at the Oxford Crown Court, from the Oxfordshire area, and appointed to the magistrate's bench.

Once we were sworn in, the magistrates were invited to attend a two-part training session. We spent a great deal of time, during the first session getting acquainted with the magistrate system. This took a few sittings, but after a while things began to fall in place. By the time the second session started, I had a much better understanding of how the judicial system works. Not all thirty-eight of us completed the training program. There were some of the candidates who experienced problems with job conflicts. By the end of the second training phase, we had all become fairly adept and competent in understanding the nuances and dynamics of being magistrates. The Banbury magistrate roll had also been increased by nine new members. One of them was John Elliot Brooks, Anguillan, carpenter, soldier, endurance walker, businessman, and politician. I accepted the post of magistrate, with all its responsibilities, and as a member of the community. I also committed to working in conjunction with others to administer justice in the community. While I was referred to in the press as "the town's first black magistrate," I saw the appointment and the experience differently. I was a black magistrate who was expected to work in conjunction with all the others, as they administered justice in the city. Once I started my term, I sat an average of twice per month, at times it was a few more sittings, depending on the availability of magistrates.

When I became part of the magistrate system, my feelings were of excitement and commitment. However, there were incidents that impacted on me negatively, as a magistrate, and caused me to become disillusioned with aspects of the justice system. For example, there were times when I thought certain cases should not have been brought to court. However, there were usually convictions, seemingly to justify such cases being brought to the magistrate system. At times, too, the outcome of cases was influenced by the type of clothing people wore and the cars they drove. Such factors should not have impacted cases; however, quite often, they were distractions that factored into how cases were resolved. Further, while the government continued to publish material in relation to colour and other forms of prejudice, in the magistrate system one realised that such claims were more election gimmicks. Often, the very persons who wrote such rules later became the greatest offenders. Another perspective was that somehow such rules just did not work.

I recall that one day, while listening to the radio, there were news broadcasts noting that senior police officers were afraid to have conflicts with members of the force who are black because of the fear they will be branded as racists. However, such incidents happen only when the officers divert from the real facts of a case to see mainly skin colour. Usually, it is in such instances that interpersonal difficulties evolve. In any situation where police officers deliberately avoid reality or act on the basis of learned false consciousness driven by prejudices, there are bound to be instances of conflicts and confrontations in the society. When officers are guilty of not accepting police recruits from non-white groups as part of their team, and such persons are treated as less than equal, this can be part of a strategy to make such minority persons uncomfortable. At that point, they may want to refuse assignments into such organisations. In that case, the leaders in the organisations will continue to harbour inner fears, while at the same time wondering why the equality matter has not been resolved in their units. The longer I remained as a magistrate in Banbury, the more frustrated I became about some of what I saw. After about nineteen years, I gave up the office and left with a sense of disappointment. I came away with hard evidence that justice is not quite blind; it often sees, even Britain.

My experiences as a magistrate brought home to me, in a practical way, that in real life "all that glitters is not necessarily gold." A study of the magistrate system may reveal some of the reasons why certain racial and cultural groups avoid joining the uniform organisations in Britain. However, that subtle resistance is not limited to uniform organisations. Equal opportunity is more readily written about than acted on, or practiced in real life situations. Some observations on racial bias were done at the factory where I worked. The results were unsettling. Twelve men were working together when an urgent order was requested. Unknown to the foreman, the only person in the group who could complete the order on time was one of the two West Indian workers at the plant. The foreman asked only the white workers whether they could complete the order. However, none of them could complete it. Eventually, the foreman was alerted as to who was competent enough to complete the job. His desperation left him no alternative, so he approached the minority worker and asked to have the work done. The Afro-Caribbean worker finished the assignment with time to spare. Notwithstanding, the foreman's bias had been exhibited to, and noted by, all the workers at the factory.

I left the office of magistrate experiencing a down mood and a solemn sense of disappointment because of some the things I experienced and saw there. However, I was never one to alienate myself from my community. What I did was to search for new ways to involve myself, especially in working with charities and to become involved with political action. As early as March 2005, I became aware that there was a citizens' movement to nominate me Mayor of the town. Despite that foreknowledge, I followed my plans and went home to Anguilla for a three-week vacation. While there, I responded to my urge and did some gardening. I would be up by 5 AM, then, did landscaping plus other aspects of gardening until about 8 AM. Early one morning, my wife phoned me in Anguilla and gave me a contact number to call back in Banbury. I gave my word that I would call, but did not follow through with the promise. At that time, I knew that once a person served as a councillor, he or she was in line and could be nominated to serve as Mayor of the town. Admittedly, it was a position that was attractive to me and I thought about it from time to time. After I left the military, I did set myself a number of possible goals still to be accomplished. It was very ambitious at the time, but one of those goals was to serve as Mayor in Banbury. Eventually, it happened. In May 2005, I was granted the singular honour of becoming Mayor of Banbury for one year, 2005-2006.

When I returned to England from Anguilla, Councillor, J. C. came to see me. It was he who had asked that I contact him from Anguilla. He wanted to talk with me about the mayoral vacancy that existed in the town. As I always did when asked to serve my community, I answered the query in the affirmative. "I would be honored to serve," I responded. There I was an Anguillan being nominated to be the Mayor of a city in Britain. After some preliminaries, and following my formal acceptance of the offer to become Mayor of Banbury, an inauguration took place at Banbury Town Council Offices on May 17, 2005. For one year, from that moment, I was the new and officially elected Mayor of Banbury. The robing ceremony took place where the chain of office and the other symbols of the office were passed to me. It was quite a humbling experience for me. My family and many good friends cheered loudly and wished me good luck. The newspapers focused on the fact that I was the first ever black Mayor in the area. However, I did not see the appointment from a stance of colour. Rather, I looked at it in terms of whether

I was competent enough to do the job, and to do it well. I had no doubt that I could!

Banbury is a somewhat conservative town. It was unusual and strange that a West Indian should be elected then as its Mayor. However, after the military, I settled in the area and had been quite open with my support for conservative politics. Notwithstanding, I was not very certain about the varied requirements for the position as Mayor. Not long after the swearing in, I was required to present a speech to the audience gathered for the ceremony. Special guests included the Lord Lieutenant of Oxfordshire, the queen's representative, the high sheriff and many more distinguished guests. As could be expected, I felt a certain anxiety about what I should present on such an auspicious occasion. However, my initial fear and concern were soon gone. My new secretary, Tricia Campbell, seemed prepared for every situation I encountered. Without much ado, she had put together my speech for the evening. After that occasion there was a year before me when I had to carry out a full program of activities. Some were routine but others had to be planned.

Maybe it was my prior experiences working with charities, but I was urged in the direction of reaching out to help young people in the area, particularly those between the ages of eight and twenty-one. Included in that interest group were talented people on both sides of the age group. Another interest was fundraising for charities, and there was a special volunteers' reception. Three charities that received my special attention were Carers West Oxfordshire, and the Citizens Advice Bureau. There were also the cheque presentation ceremonies. Some of the charities I was directly acquainted with and had served on their boards. My inaugural evening went quite well. There were moments of thrill, excitement, and surprises. One event that stood out, and which was very special and meaningful for me, was the reading of a letter sent in my honour by the government and people of Anguilla. It was a very pleasant surprise for me. The ceremony came to a close after a very warm and momentous reception.

Tricia Campbell held the post of secretary to the Mayor for a very long time. During the period, she made many contacts and built good relationships within the community. Because she was well known, Tricia Campbell had easy access to schools, businesses, churches, charities, volunteer workers, and various clubs. The knowledge and experience of Tricia Campbell made it very easy for me to prepare a programme and set goals for my office, then we had to work effectively at achieving them during the year. There were many things that stood out for me during my year as the Mayor of Banbury. One event that comes to mind was the fifteenth anniversary of the hospice opening. It was an ongoing project. We worked on the exterior of the building and refurbished the in-patient unit. That included the replacement of carpets, curtains, linens, and furniture. The refurbishing process included the upholstering of large sofa chairs, a major part of the project laid out for the year. The overall cost of that upgrade to the hospice was in excess of fifty thousand pounds.

I was never a person to sit back and wait for things to happen. In such a situation, one can be passed over and left out of the important action. Rather than becoming a victim to such a situation, I always looked for opportunities to act preemptively, a strategy that became very useful to me while I served as Mayor. There were certain established duties, but no specific agenda as to how one should or should not act during the year as Mayor. Further, since I was the first Afro-Caribbean person to serve in the office as Mayor in Banbury, the challenge to be successful and creative in the position was somewhat daunting. However, I never saw it as something beyond my ability or experience.

One factor that favoured my leadership at the time was that by 2005 to 2006, the population of Banbury had grown and changed considerably. There was an unprecedented influx of East Europeans and Asians. With that in mind, one thing I did was to organise the first inter-cultural fair. In my planning of events, I capitalised on the new ethnic and cultural diversity in the area. There were functions on different evenings to greet and welcome persons from the varied cultural backgrounds in the community. It was also arranged for different leaders from the community and community organisations to address the new-comers and explain how the social and political systems into which they had just entered work. I also moved to promote the town by inviting town mayors from throughout the area, Oxfordshire, Buckinghamshire, Warwickshire and Northamptonshire, to join us in our festive events. My effort turned out to be a very successful venture. It helped the different communities to come together and experience harmony, despite their differences.

The annual town criers' competition now held in Banbury developed as a result of my effort to bring together the different people and cultures in the area in a friendly but competitive manner. There were many other memorable events and occasions during my year as Mayor. I recall that we had tea and dinner dances. There were the usual charity events, including collecting toys for children, a bazaar, and efforts to expand the volunteer force in the community. We celebrated VE Day. The cattle market development programme was a special agricultural activity. Students from Japan were invited to visit Banbury. Our 40th year of having Craft Food in Banbury occasioned a town-wide celebration. We celebrated the 65th anniversary of the Air Training Corps (ATC), the Royal Air Force Association in the area, dating back to 1941 and WW II. More than seventy past and present members participated in that ACT event. There was also quite some pomp and show for the 220th anniversary celebration for Lord Nelson's finest hour. As part of the commemoration of that famous British victory at sea, ten English oaks were planted in Spiceball Park. The tree idea was the brain child of Sir Philip Watson of Bodicote. Banbury's Chestnut Bowls Club also held its 225th anniversary, during that year. There was our Remembrance Day celebration and a special ceremony to highlight Banbury's Canal Day. Also, no one will soon forget that special Caribbean evening held January 20th, 2006. It was another of the first time events celebrated during my year as Mayor. I referred to the ceremony as "Banbury's One and Only Caribbean Evening." Actually, it was my attempt to help the people forget their winter blues. My intention that January night was to whisk them away to the fantasy of the sunny and warm Caribbean. The special ceremony was held in the town hall and went from 7:30 PM till midnight. The programme included a buffet of Caribbean foods. There was rum punch, live Caribbean music, including steel-band and calypsos. It would not be a Caribbean evening if it did not include the limbo dance—a dance I participated in quite happily. It all brought back fond memories of warm and happy times in the Caribbean. For those who could not attend the Caribbean Night event, they were offered an opportunity to purchase tickets for ten pounds and win a two-week Caribbean vacation in Anguilla. The whole affair was an exciting and memorable way to showcase the Caribbean, and to introduce other dimensions of Caribbean people and culture to the community of Banbury.

There were also other social dimensions to my year as Mayor. I oversaw the start of a 320-unit estate housing project. There were concerns about violence in the community, and I endeavoured to help resolve some of the problems. One of my strategies was to direct the youths towards alternative or different activities with which to engage their lives. Among my suggested alternatives were that they joined churches, community organisations, the navy, the army, and the air force. I was also able to speak directly to them about how the military impacted my life. Getting the youths involved in fundraising and other positive activities, instead of vandalism, was always a critical thrust during my mayoral year. As I ended my term as Mayor, I was moved to comment on the "courtesy and manners of the young people in Banbury." It was also during my tenure that Banbury accepted the challenge and stepped-up to become a fair-trade town. We were one of the early communities across Britain that pledged to help third-world communities earn decent living opportunities by regular purchase of fair-trade products from poorer countries around the world.

At the end of the year, I turned over the mayor's office to John Donaldson. He was a twenty-year resident of Banbury and had been a town councillor for two years. I recall that the newspaper suggested he had two challenges as he took over from me. One was to keep his weight at a reasonable level. He was threatened with a fine of ten pounds for each pound he gained during the year. The next challenge he had was to innovate and achieve at the same level that I did during the year I served. In that year, I attended 400 scheduled visits, raised over ten thousand pounds for forty-two charities, and organised a variety of events to help promote the well-being of the Banbury community.

By the time I ended my tenure as Mayor on May 22, 2006, it was evident to me that where one starts life it never has to end there. I was going home again, for the third time in twenty-two years. Each of my work experiences, as soldier, as businessman, and as politician, has helped to shape my life and moved it into directions I never dreamed about before. The opportunity to emigrate from Anguilla to Britain changed my life and being in fundamental ways. I am not the person I dreamed of becoming before I left Anguilla and came to England in 1955. My having come to England has changed my life in ways I continue to reflect on, and of which I am proud. Generally, I like the *me* I have become, during the past forty-five years. I am different from what I dreamed I would be. But I am still me. And I do enjoy living with the "me" I have become. As the song made famous by Frank Sinatra noted, when I reflect on my life, the "regrets are few." However, I can never proclaim that I lived my life my way. As I reflect on where I have been, it is very obvious; the circumstances that surround my migration from Anguilla to Britain worked to shape what my life has become. It may not have been all my way, but the experiences have been wonderful to me.

NEITHROP WARD

CHERWELL DISTRICT
COUNCIL ELECTION

I'm sorry you were out when I called today. I look forward to meeting you soon.

If you have any problems contact me at 16a North Bar, Banbury, or phone me on 62341 or 53825.

John Brooks

My Political Calling Card

Mayor of Banbury 2006

Mayor of Banbury 2006

Mayoral Activities-Toys For The Children

Mayoral Activities-Toys For The Children

Mayor Brooks Dancing the Limbo

Mayoral Activities- A Parade

Front card -1

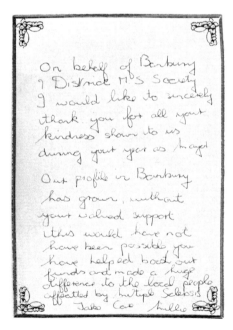

Inside card-1

Front card-2 copy

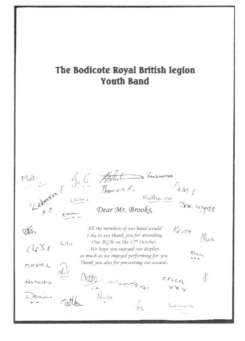

Inside card-2

Mayoral Activities- Meeting Anguilla's Athletic Team

Mayoral Activities-Anguilla Team 1976 Commonwealth 2002

Mayor Brooks With Secretary Patricia Campbell-2006

Canal Day My Year As Major 2005 to 2006

Attending Official Ceremony

Final Function- Other Mayors and Queen's Rep

Chapter Ten

Looking Back Over My Life

Today, I am no longer the gung-ho soldier or the daring endurance walker of the 1970s and 1980s. Such events took place at another time and during an earlier point in my life. After twenty-six years with the military, about ten tough years as an endurance walker, and another nineteen years in business, I am now a happily retired senior citizen. However, like most sane human beings, I, too, pause frequently and reflect on my life. I take the time to ponder deliberately on where my life has been, how I got there, and how far I have come since my early years as a boy going to school and growing up in Anguilla.

Back then, my sister Ruby teased and called me a "duncy head." She was sure I would not go very far in life, intellectually or otherwise. At that time, too, life in Anguilla promised a very limited future unless one had done well in school. But I was not excited about school, and my academic performance told a story of struggle, as I worked through my classes, without interest or excitement. My options were to become an apprentice to some tradesman, or since migration was popular at that time, maybe my family would agree to my moving elsewhere to try my hand at starting over away from Anguilla. While my mother and father did all they could to nurture me and make me comfortable, my other family members were aware that I did not do very well in school, but in my family, academic performance mattered. Seemingly, my sisters and brothers expected little from me in terms of my life beyond the walls of the school I attended in Anguilla. Maybe that factor was one reason why my parents provided me an early opportunity for migration far away. They were probably hoping I could find a niche to serve as a hiding place for me in Britain. Whatever the original plan was, in my family, that early move to Britain became a revolutionary and transformational force in my life. It changed my aspirations and transformed my very being. Some of the changes that came to my life were so pervasive that in time, I proved my sister's anticipation for my future to be wrong. It also demonstrated that no human being is inherently and forever less than another. There is always that inward potential for future development. I have learned that very often, it is the opportunities to which persons are exposed in life that can make the difference in terms of who they become. Those opportunities also determine the quality of footprints left on the sands of one's time in this life.

My early experiences in Anguilla coupled with the opportunities I had for learning and growth in Britain combined to ensure me a good life. It has been much different from that I would have lived if the opportunities available to me in Anguilla were all that I had known throughout my life. Probably, much of my early life was scripted, and a function of my colonial experience, having been born in the British colony of St. Kitts, Nevis, and Anguilla. Growing up there in the early 1900s was quite a limiting experience. From as far back as the 1800s, emigration was viewed by the citizenry as a path by which to escape a life on the islands—a life punctuated with drudgery and islandism. It was a secure but monotonous life for most West Indians. At a time when the world was rushing into the twentieth century, life on the West Indian islands was increasingly a very limiting experience for most young West Indians. As Wardle (2004) argued, emigration is an escape strategy from one's birth island in the Caribbean. It is usually an adventure, moving from one's island usually strangled by poverty, while at the same time struggling with limited education and powerlessness among the people. When the migrant adventurer arrives in that other place, the new experience stimulates the human desire for adventure, may also encourage anonymity, while allowing unprecedented opportunities for personal growth change and development. Accordingly, when I entered into that other cultural reality, there were aspects of my life which suddenly became unscripted. They took me by surprise. The dreams I built for myself as a boy in Anguilla suddenly had limited meaning. They had been shaped largely by my experiences on a small, colonised Caribbean island, still somewhat alienated and on the periphery of the wider world. Those dreams were carved from the Caribbean reality of the 1940s and 1950s. Independent thinking back then was discouraged in the islands and treated as a radical idea to be suppressed and discouraged. When one grew up on a colonised island there was a tendency to see the world through dependent controlled perspectives, a view of the world shaped largely by false consciousness.

Accordingly, when I left Anguilla for Britain in 1955, at age twenty, I knew very little then about how the world I was leaving and the one I was about to enter differed. Neither did I have a clue as to how that difference between them would change both my reality and my dreams. For example, entry into the British military, as I did in 1958, was never part of my life's plan. I wanted to work for a few years, then return to Anguilla permanently. Notwithstanding, that unexpected turn in my life impacted both my experiences and my development. A liberation and broadening came to my life after I moved from the Caribbean to live in England. I was also instructed daily, as never before, about the vicissitudes and unpredictability of the human life. Matters of culture shock, the shifting human reality, and about the meaning of one's life, were also brought into focus; as I grappled with, and learned about life beyond my colonial experience back in Anguilla. It was like the birth of a new self, ideologically and otherwise.

Up until 1955, I could not see myself living any place else but Anguilla, for very long. I hardly even imagined it. For me, Anguilla with its warm sunshine, predictable weather condition, and enchanting beaches, was the perfect place to live. Eventually, however, I agreed to slip away for a while. I intended to come back home and live, for the rest of my life, in my beloved island. However, once I ventured beyond Anguilla, the liberating instructions and the accompanying independent experiences caused me to make big changes to my plans. Now, I am not certain whether I should call Anguilla or Britain home, or in which place I really want to be, as I face my end-time. And that is only a small part of how my emigration experience changed my expectations and shaped who and what I have become.

While I have occasionally thought back and asked whether I did the right thing when I opted out of my business in 2003, today, there are no second thoughts as to whether I did the right thing when I moved from the Caribbean to see what life for me would be in Britain. As a soldier in the British military, I fell in love with the challenges of the martial experience. Because I enjoyed the experiences and appreciated how they were transforming my life, I committed myself to a step-up process that earned me recognition in varied forms, first in the military and then in civilian life. Actually, it was because I was at home with soldiering why I agreed to serve as long as I did. From time to time, I do reflect on my service in the military and the numerous awards I received for excellence. I have also kept newspaper clippings and pictures that reflect or comment on my commendations through those twenty-six years of my soldiering.

The commendations included special recognition with the rest of my platoon after my first six weeks in the military. Later I was given a special award by Queen Elizabeth II, many years before I met her in person. Other awards and recognition came from my superior officers in the military. There were also honours and recognition from my peers in civilian life, including the government and organisations from Anguilla. There are persons who also continue to suggest that, despite the fact that it was a unique and unusual experience for me, my tenure as Mayor in Banbury was quite a memorable one. It was punctuated by different and interesting cultural events, some of which have been institutionalised since my term of service. The very large attendance at the event marking my final function in office as Mayor was referred to by many persons as an indication of the high esteem in which I was held by the community. My involvement with charities was also an important feature during the year as Mayor, as was the case during my military and civilian life. There are many persons from businesses, charitable organisations, schools, colleges, and churches, whom I still thank for their courtesies and generosity during my mayoral year. I was privileged to distribute some forty-three cheques to various charities. Through the years, I still continue to appreciate the honour to have come from one of the tiniest islands in the Caribbean and be elected to such a prestigious position, to serve as the Mayor of a town in Britain. Such an achievement was never among my initial dreams, but because of my new experiences in Britain, it became one of the accomplishments that I will always treasure dearly in my lifetime. During that year, I also had the honour to officiate at almost 300 official and non-official visits that many persons paid to Banbury.

I also travelled around and saw much of the wider world, while I served in the British military. During that time, I started to understand and appreciate more than before what it means to give so that less fortunate persons in this world can be helped. While I was in the military, I had the opportunity to visit a number of countries and islands, including Germany, Belgium, Holland, France, Norway, Denmark, Singapore, Malaysia, Brunei, Hong Kong, China, Malta, Canada, USA, Thailand, Turkey, and other West Indian islands besides Anguilla, that I knew little about before I left for Britain During those visits, I saw life at its best in some places and at its worst in others. From time to time, I was challenged to reflect on an earlier period of my life back in Anguilla. I still cannot forget how the Canadian Government and people reached out to us, on more than one occasion. The numerous and timely gifts from Canada were useful to aid and succour my island. Those gifts ensured the survival and well-being of many persons on Anguilla back then.

There was also the girl I had loved back in Anguilla, before I left for Britain. I still recall our meetings at the Methodist Church where we attended together. It was a very painful parting for both of us, so we made each other endearing promises. However, they were promises which time and circumstances did not allow either of us to keep. My dream was that we would get married one day and spend the rest of our life, living happily together in Anguilla. However, those dreams were derailed by the twists and turns of life. They never came true. I left and went to live thousands of miles away in England. My then girlfriend later moved to St. Kitts-Nevis as a teacher. She married a businessman who later became a politician in Nevis. I in turn met Audrey, a nurse, and the rest is history. Fate did not bring me and my Anguillan girl together as we dreamed. Time and circumstances intervened and kept us apart. They pushed our lives in other directions.

Instead of an Anguillan, I am married to Audrey from St. Kitts. I met her in England during the late 1950s after she came to England as a nursing student. Today, she is still my very special and favourite nurse. We now have three children and two grandchildren. Through the years, they have all been there to stand with and by me. My family has provided rock-like support for me, and has helped as I worked my way through both happy and through difficult times. They accompanied me around the world while I served as a soldier. In particular, they were there with me during those difficult and stressful and weary days of endurance walking. There was never a success that my family did not share with me during my walking years. They also shared my painful times. . I could never have attained where I reached without them being there for me. The military also played a critical role in my walking career. Quite often it was my supporters from the military, who spurred me on in the endurance competitions and made my many successes possible. That was especially true those times when my being was barely coherent and operated at the edge of insanity.

After being away from Anguilla for forty years, my initial dream to build a house on the island came to fruition. Years ago when I left the island, I was alone and thinking only of myself. My parents and I thought that being able to build a house to live in and probably raise a family should be my priority for life. Back then, I thought so, too. However, many changes have come to my life since then but building that house in Anguilla remained an important matter to me. Today, I am able to say that I made the promise and then kept it.

Since I now have a family, the house I built is larger than originally planned. It is much more than a building just for me. Probably, I was thinking of not being selfish, and wanted to build something that can accommodate my children and grandchildren too. I have found it interesting, but in England and in Anguilla, when I discuss my thinking about property, I have been ridiculed as foolish. Some persons think that children should be given an education then left to fend for themselves, finding their own way in life. While I agree that education is important, from my experience, I do not see anything wrong with giving one's children a start in life, beyond an education, if that is financially possible. My parents were not able to do that for me, but they did what they could. They gave me an education, then a ticket to England. It was a ticket that allowed me a passage to another world. That other world I have come to know is very different from what my parents lived in and knew.

On my later return trips to Anguilla, I discovered that the island has progressed considerably. It also seems to have been lengthened by at least one mile, since my days of growing up there. When I went to school, I was taught that the island was 3 miles wide and 15 miles long. Today we are told it is still 3 miles wide and 16 miles long. That is unlike Nevis, which at one time was listed as being 50 square miles in size, now the island is supposedly 36 square miles. While Anguilla gained one mile Nevis lost 14 square miles.

Since I had no idea what the future held for me, I underestimated how long it would take before I would return and build my house in Anguilla. Many of us who travelled from the West Indies in the 1950s had no picture of how migrating to England would change our worldview and who we could become. Some of us managed to return to our islands, although not in five years time as planned; others remained undecided about whether to return, and there have been those who, sadly, will never return to the Caribbean again. They did not survive their journey beyond the islands.

In my case, the Brooks family has been well known in Anguilla for a long time, so I have very deep roots there. I have visited whenever possible, and on a regular basis made charitable contributions to the public hospital and to other worthy entities. Further, because of my special linkages to Anguilla, there has e been more than one Anguillan whom I assisted in attaining academic qualifications and success in Britain. This was not done with the aim of impressing anyone. I did it because I find pleasure in helping people in need when I can and from time to time I came into contact with young Anguillans who needed that assistance. There is a certain intrinsic satisfaction I get from helping others in this life. As a result, when I wake up in the morning and draw the curtains, I always see some sun shining through my life, even when it is a rainy or cloudy day. At times, I walk through the garden and around the house. I look at my picture collection on the walls, too; and they bring back powerful memories. Sometimes too, I would look at where I am, contemplate where I came from, and think about my next move in life — where I can still go and find some challenge to conquer.

It would not be fair if I wrote this book and failed to pay tribute to a fellow Anguillan, who was a special friend and colleague, Mr. Alfred Gumbs. We left Anguilla at the same time to travel to England and arrived here on the same ship in 1955. Since Alfred was older and more seasoned to the sea than I was, he did not experience the severe sea-sickness that I did. Consequently, he comforted and cared for me throughout the eleven-day journey. Alfred was always a generous man. He never allowed his family to interfere with his generosity, when there was a situation requiring him to help others. Mr. Gumbs was careful to help young people, too. He would often spend time encouraging them to attend university as part of their planning for the future. Usually, Gumbs provided help as his friends needed it. Some of the youths received Mr. Gumbs's verbal assistance while others got financial assistance. There were cases where certain students did not heed the wisdom gained with age. Some also set off in directions which turned out to be disappointing later in life. . However, some of those young people did get to the point where they turned around, came into their own, and found a new self. There were also those who turned around and in time, became competent professionals and mentors to others. This short poem was written in memory of, and as a tribute to my late friend, Alfred Gumbs. He is one of the many Caribbean migrants who stayed in England.

> *I think of you weekly as though you were still here,*
> *Remembering the times we had together at sea and on land,*
> *How we worked together, you were in the dirt, and I in the sand,*
> *Brice Field in Maidenhead will always be remembered,*
> *For giving us our first job in this wonderful land.*

If someone would ask me today, "Where is your home?" I will say England. But if someone asks, "Where are you from?" I will say Anguilla, West Indies. As cynical as this may appear, I have lived here for most of my life and understand the basic workings of the country. That does not mean that I have forgotten my roots, because I do continue to love the island of Anguilla and to appreciate the indelible memories I hold of my early life there. Notwithstanding, today, after spending about four or five weeks visiting Anguilla, I seem to experience an overwhelming urge to return to England. It becomes more powerful than the desire to remain in Anguilla. I guess this reality leaves my situation open for the suggestion, "You have given up the place where you were born for another country."But, there is another way of seeing my situation. I have come to love both places.

However, while I was born in Anguilla, it was in England where I really grew up, learned about the world, and came into my own as a man. Despite some limiting factors, I have done well in England. Through the years, I had exposure to, and opportunities for personal development here that I could have only dreamed about in the Caribbean. I can truly say that I became most of what I am because I migrated to Britain. After I arrived here, I discovered that the world is much larger than the one I knew before. I also discovered that there is much more to life than just building and owning a house. Further, while I managed successfully to surmount some racial and cultural barriers in Britain, the class and political barriers to success in Anguilla could have also dwarfed my life. Over time, I have come to learn that these y are there, and very present in the society. Even when vacancies existed, there would be no guarantee that I could have interviewed and got the jobs I wanted. Despite the danger and hardships inherent in the military life, I survived all twenty-six years of it, and, in time, I have become a bigger and better person.

During one trip to Anguilla, I recall visiting a particular shop. To my surprise, one of the shop's assistants said to me, "You people go to England with nothing and come back with nothing." Although the comment was interesting, it was also a big lie. . I came back from England with an education that gave me a better understanding of the world. My experiences show that West Indians can live their dreams and rise to the top in Britain. I also came back from England knowing that being in the military is a worthwhile, growth-promoting experience, and ultimately an enjoyable career. Just as it happens when one is living the civilian life, there are similar stresses and heartaches in the military. As a soldier, I was empowered to evaluate situations, make up my mind about them, and act independently to enhance my survival success. I was also able to earn the money so that I could return to Anguilla with confidence and some financial independence, to build the house in Anguilla, as I had promised my parents and myself.

There were also some other concerns I had about my fellow Anguillans. Through the years, I have had opportunities to affiliate with companies, charities, and a wide range of organisations run by persons from other countries. However, when I dealt with Anguillan organisations in Britain and expected high moral principles, at times I became very disappointed. For example, the Anguillan Association in Britain could have been a strong and progressive association because it had a good start, as early as back in the 1950s. However, when the organization should have stabilized, as we moved into the 1970s and 1980s, the leaders started to lose sight of their objectives. The success of the individual started to take precedence over the welfare and success of the group. My involvement with the military limited my idea about an early membership in the organisation. Later, when I lived at Banbury, about 68 miles return from Slough, Mr. Claude Brooks, MBE, chair of the association, sent me regular invitations to the Association's activities. They included meetings, the visits of Anguillan dignitaries, and other special events. During my attendance at such events, I started to deduce that the organisation was in trouble and on the verge of collapse. Something about it seemed very wrong to me.

When Claude Brooks invited me to assist in getting the Anguillan organisation reorganised, I agreed to help. We had a meeting and a committee was formed. I soon realised that the failure of the organisation was due to mismanagement, particularly of its funds. Since I was nominated to be treasurer, I started my review of things by examining the books carefully. I learned that there were many irregularities involving the funds for the organisation. Accordingly, I brought the matter to the attention of the chairman. Some of the irregularities brought to light included dealings in a variety of matters. One was a situation where shares at a business had been bought in the name of the association, but for a particular individual.

However, none of the executives remembered or knew anything about shares having been bought for the organization back in 1988. It was discovered that the treasurer of the Association then was a Mr. E. R. However, it happened that there were two Anguillans by the same name, Mr. E. R. When I started my investigation, I questioned the wrong Mr. E. R. It was he who led me to the real Mr. E. R. The correct Mr. E. R. was very aggressive and threatening when he was first located and confronted about the matter. My next step was to remind him that we grew up together on the same island and that his actions were contrary to the values we inherited and learned in Anguilla. During a future meeting about the shares, it was pointed out to Mr. E. R. that all the documents related to the shares and dividends were made out in his name and to his address. There were some dividends that were not cashed, but there was also evidence from the accounting records that no dividends had been paid to the accounts for the shares.

In a further meeting which should have been private, Mr. E. R. was so certain of himself that he brought along about four of his friends for support and evidence. However, when I produced and shared the documents, Mr. E. R's friends were shocked to learn the extent to which he had cheated the Association. Once his scheming was exposed, Mr. E. R. could do little more than confess his guilt. He also promised to explain his actions to the Association. Accordingly, another meeting was arranged. Unfortunately, Mr. E. R. did not present any details about the missing funds. Interestingly, he was also very involved with the affairs of his church, but had managed quite well to hide his dishonesty for a number of years.

A further expression of dishonesty was noted later, when I tried to do some business in Anguilla. I found that many of the representatives for Anguilla, from varied levels of the society, would visit England and make beautiful promises, to persons making enquiries about business possibilities in Anguilla. Quite often those promises amounted to little more than hot air. I observed over time, as was the case with Mr. E. R, that many islanders took part in actions that were in direct conflict with their religious and cultural realities . Seemingly, the exposure of Anguillans to increased materialism brought many contradictions to their lives about values and making choices in life. Often, I found it more productive to deal with professionals in Britain than with professionals in Anguilla. There were many situations where I experienced very little sincere engagement from the Anguillans. Very often there were members of the social and political elite on the island, who pushed others around in an uncalled for manner. Then, there was also the bad habit where Anguillan leaders would agree to appointments to see visitors, then, on arriving for the appointments, the person who agreed to the appointments was not available because he had to leave the island suddenly. Unfortunately, in the world beyond Anguilla, such unreliable behaviour is seen as poor business practice. Such actions must be addressed and changed if the island is to continue showing true progress. These are times of dynamism and creativity and even islands such as Anguilla must step-up. The old bureaucratic way of doing things, a hold-over from the colonial era, must be changed. Anguillans today have to learn and grow from a different, less constricting experience.

Since I spent so many years in the military, there may be persons thinking that I have lots of buddies from friendships developed during those years. However, the corps to which I was attached had the policy of moving the men around after every two years. In the final analysis, the men remained little more than acquaintances during the time they were in the military together. From time to time, I did try to pursue certain friendships with other soldiers, but my efforts were never very successful. Maybe my lack of deep, long-term friendships, with males, over the years, was related to my early school days in Anguilla. Back then, I was very comfortable being alone. As time went by and I got older, my being alone seems to allow me time to think deeply and to formulate new ideas. At times, I also became very interested in pursuing and preserving the privacy of such times. Over the years I have tried hard to continue pursuing them. During those military years, Lieutenant Colonel John Connelly became a tower of strength in my life. That was despite the difference in our ranking. We were good friends for many of those years. He trusted my ability and often made certain that the jobs I was assigned allowed me some form of recognition for my performance. We organised a number of charitable affairs together. Over time, I did achieve worthwhile military recognition and other lasting benefits.

Another person I considered an important male friend was Roger Evans; he was a manager of the Midland Bank. It was very evident that Mr. Evans went beyond the call of duty to help me meet my financial needs as I struggled to set up my business. After his retirement, Mr. Evans and I remained in contact. Occasionally, we went out for meals because of the respect we shared for each other and the value we attached to our friendship. Today, among my male friends is my solicitor, Gavin Lloyd, Ll.B (Dub), whom I have known since 1971. It has been a great pleasure working with him through the years. There is also my bank manager, who has become a good, dependable friend. Another one of my few friends is Mike Howes, an ex-military man and an accountant. We met first by accident, but through the years I came to depend on him quite heavily. There was also my faithful handyman, Henry Doway. He was someone whom I turned to for assistance for many years until he retired in 2003. Henry was such a reliable and faithful friend. Some of the men I hang out and knock around with these days are not really persons with whom I have deep, long-lasting friendships. As fate would have it, many of my close friends are women, some are married while others are single. Most of them are persons I met during my military years. Not all of these women reside in Britain or in Anguilla. They are wide ranging in their countries of origin, race, and culture.

Some of these persons and I are not in contact regularly, however, special occasions are always remembered. That, to me, is part of what true friendships are about. These are persons who aided my career and development in some way. I can still call upon many of them at times when I have need for assistance. Quite often I depended on these friends to help me achieve my varied objectives in life. Interestingly, there are some of these persons whom I have never met. Our interactions have been limited to telephone conversations. Meanwhile, I cannot think of too many male contacts with whom I related as well, or at the same level of trust and friendship. At times, my entire family benefitted from these relationships. Over time, I did loose contact with some of the persons referred to here. Such long-term relationships also become subjected to the stresses and changes in life. However, when I reflect on all the persons who touched my life and helped to give it meaning, through the years, I still get vivid pictures of many dear friends from around the world, who were there for me at the varied stages of my life. Very pleasant memories do come fleeting back to my mind.

True, there have been times when I looked back over my life and wished I had gone further, or achieved more, personally, during my lifetime. However, I often console myself with the thought that my life's journey started in lowly Anguilla, and since that time, I rose to challenges which helped me to rise and soar beyond that "duncy head" label with which my sister branded me, so many years ago. Had I remained in Anguilla, how very much that could have limited my life is an unanswered question. Indeed, the soars I made through the years and the dreams that came to inspire me, or the reaches I attained in my life, were "not attained by sudden flight." Every step towards the successes I achieved was a challenge, a struggle, and required determination. At times the fact that I came through as well as I did amazes even me. The patterning to my life has been that as I realised the fulfillment of one dream, there were always those others which kept coming to my mind. However, despite an opportunity for a liberating renewal process in one's life. No human being has time on his or her side forever. We become old worn out, and in time lose the drive of youth. Through the years I observed it in the experience of others. Now, I have come to feel and experience it for myself. Eventually, I heeded my better judgment and started listening to those messengers inside my being.

While there are still some occasional feelings of restlessness accompanied by insane urges to do daring activities. Today I no longer entertain thoughts of invincibility. I am now really retired. Each day I feel and understand better the growing limits of my body. Yet, suddenly, I have the time to do things I could not do before, and there are temptations. However, despite the cost to my pride, I now take care to slow down, pause, observe, enjoy and smell the flowers that now come to my life, as it meanders on gently. There are those times, too, when I pause deliberately, sit back, and reflect on all that my life has been. One of the things I still continue to dream about today is that young people who have experienced poverty and powerlessness, particularly those from the Caribbean area, can examine my life's experiences and find new meaning for their own. They can learn from another person's use of determination, commitment, and will to survive. I learned firsthand, and do not doubt that life can become an interesting adventure, providing a variety of opportunities if young people have the willingness to venture out, learn, and grow, from dreams. They can transform lives. That has been very much a part of my unusual story. Consequently, my special message to everyone is that all human beings have the capacity to step-up, learn, grow, and at times change an initially perceived destiny. There are many more opportunities and paths to success available today than were there when I was growing up. However, I accepted the opportunities that came my way and used them to transform my life. Such an approach to life may not necessarily be easier, but it still remains possible and more viable today, even in the Caribbean area.

Despite my more relaxed life today, a time in my life when I am no longer hyped up and on the run, it does not mean that I pine, howl, or think as if all my adventures are over. I continue to remain positive, and "keep on keeping on." At times, I visit residential homes for senior citizens, and I enjoy collecting clocks. Some time is also spent building up my stamp and coin collections. Also, from time to time, I visit the sergeant's mess at the nearby military complex, where I meet old friends and acquaintances. My honourary membership there is for life and I am still very much alive.

Once, while at the ex-servicemen's club, I actually encountered His Royal Highness, The Prince of Wales, at an official tea engagement. The event was well attended and we spent time exchanging notes. When the conversation switched to Anguilla, I indicated that it is my home island, then, named my relatives there. Prince Charles noted that he had been to the island and actually had tea with my sister Nurse Vida Lloyd. However, not all my time is spent at the club. Since I enjoy travelling, from time to time, I do visit Anguilla, the US Virgin Islands, and elsewhere in the Caribbean. Such experiences help to ensure that I continue to learn and to grow. I am still alive and still very curious.

One of the conclusions I have come to accept is that experiences and cultures are master shapers of human destiny. In the process of my leaving Anguilla and seeing the world, all the related experiences and cultural encounters transformed my life. Despite the culture changes, the harsh experience of the military, and all the other challenges I met and surmounted, I still say it has been a good life! At times, I still seem to hear those words my father said to me, just before I left Anguilla for England, "Son, I do not want you to live like I have had to live, or do the jobs which I have had to do. Go away and better yourself." That was my father's dream for me. He wanted me to experience a very different life from what he knew in Anguilla. My father's counsel and dream stayed with me through all these years. It became an ideology, a philosophy, and a driving force to my life. Today, I wish my father was still around. I would go to Anguilla, visit him, or maybe take him to my house there. Time would be spent talking with him about my life and experiences since leaving the island in 1955. After all this, I would remind him about our last conversation before I left for England. Then, following all our discussions, I would ask him, "Dad, how did I do?"

Acknowledgements

A special vote of thanks for family and friends, to my wife, Audrey Brooks, Grace Lord, Ann Sewell, Elaine Davis, Christabel Connor, Dr. Richard Lloyd, my sister Audrey Brooks, , J.P., Mr. C.B. Brooks, MBE, and Miss Rosa Newlands, who have all helped me in different ways both at home and abroad.

A vote of thanks to Mr. Roger Evans, bank manager, for his advice and guidance on financial matters and whose motto to me was, "Remain on your own once the business started, for if things go wrong, there would be only one person to blame."

Mr. Gavin Lloyd L.I.B., M.A. (Dub.), my legal advisor who was always willing to offer his help at short notice and whom I have known since 1971, during the period of time when there were numerous legal issues, but nothing was ever too difficult for him.

Michael Howes, FCA, Chartered Certified Accountant, has been very helpful to me over the years, and he probably found it difficult to work with me too. My demands on him were constant, but he never let me down.

Retired Lieutenant Colonel John Connelly has been a tower of strength during my military days in spite our separation by the rank structure. We were friends for many years. If I did some special duty, or participated in an unusual assignment, he always made sure that these received recognition. Together we have organised a number of memorable charitable events, all of which turned out to be successful. To all these many persons who touched and helped to shape my life, I am forever grateful. Thank you all so very much!

John E. Brooks, BEM.

Appendix

Telegrams, Letters, Charts-, Certificates

Certificate of Merit awarded to:

_____ _Sgt J. B. Brooks_ _____

The welfare of many is in your hands – you walked to help them.

By participating in the New Territories Walk 1977–78 of the Community Chest of Hong Kong and completing the full distance, you played an important role in helping 72 Member Agencies of the Chest to assist one and a half million of Hong Kong's citizens who are in need of social welfare assistance.

Therefore, on behalf of the Chest's 72 Member Agencies, and their beneficiaries, may we express to you our appreciation and thanks.

Mrs. Siu Hon-Sum	A.K. Chui	M.C. Illingworth
Chairman	Chairman	Chairman
Campaign Committee	Walks For Millions	New Territories Walk

Certificate

Certificate of Merit awarded to:

_____ _Sgt J. B. Brooks_ _____

The welfare of many is in your hands – you walked to help them.

By participating in the New Territories Walk 1977–78 of the Community Chest of Hong Kong and completing the full distance, you played an important role in helping 72 Member Agencies of the Chest to assist one and a half million of Hong Kong's citizens who are in need of social welfare assistance.

Therefore, on behalf of the Chest's 72 Member Agencies, and their beneficiaries, may we express to you our appreciation and thanks.

Mrs. Siu Hon-Sum	A.K. Chui	M.C. Illingworth
Chairman	Chairman	Chairman
Campaign Committee	Walks For Millions	New Territories Walk

Certificate 4x6

Certificate

Walk Around the Clock

organised by

Composite Ordnance Depot

Hong Kong Stadium 1st and 2nd April 1978

CERTIFICATE

This is to certify that: SSgt. John Brooks BEM, RAOC

Team: Individual

Walked: 101 *miles* 1473 *yards*

Committee Chairman

Chief Timekeeper

Walk Official

Certificate

144

Certificate

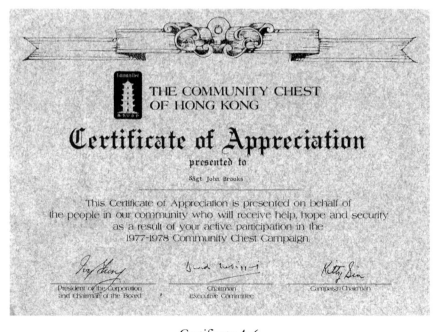

Certificate 4x6

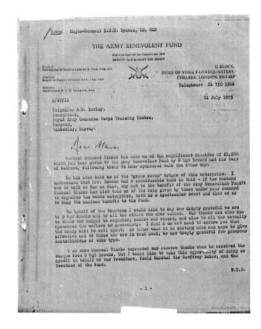

Document 1

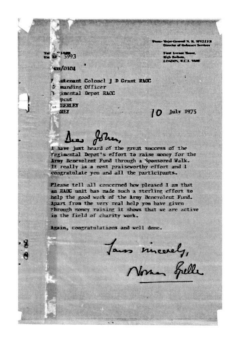

Document 1a

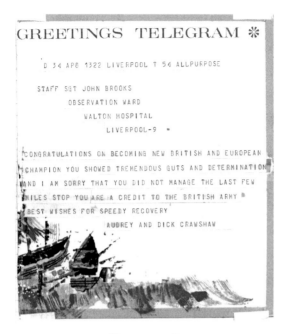

GREETINGS TELEGRAM ✳

D 34 APS 1322 LIVERPOOL T 54 ALLPURPOSE

STAFF SGT JOHN BROOKS
    OBSERVATION WARD
        WALTON HOSPITAL
            LIVERPOOL-9 =

CONGRATULATIONS ON BECOMING NEW BRITISH AND EUROPEAN
CHAMPION YOU SHOWED TREMENDOUS GUTS AND DETERMINATION
AND I AM SORRY THAT YOU DID NOT MANAGE THE LAST FEW
MILES STOP YOU ARE A CREDIT TO THE BRITISH ARMY
BEST WISHES FOR SPEEDY RECOVERY
                    AUDREY AND DICK CRAWSHAW

Document 2

From: Lieutenant Colonel C.M.G HENDY OBE RAOC   Army School of Ammunition
                                                       Temple Herdewyke
                                                       Leamington Spa
                                                       Warwickshire
                                                       CV33 0UL

                                                       Kineton Mil or
                                                       0926 640 331 ext. 380

ASA 3/24/4

WO2 J E Brooks BEM
Army School of Ammunition
Temple Herdewyke
Leamington Spa
Warwickshire
CV33 0UL   7 June 1982

Dear Mr Brooks,

        Just a short personal note to thank you for all your ideas
and hardwork that you put into our Royal display.

        As you know it was a tremendous success and there is
absolutely no doubt in my mind that your personal effort, the
firm control you exercised over all your subordinate staff and
the keen interest that you took in the whole project, paid
dividends on the day.

        I very much hope that both you and Mrs Brooks enjoyed the
day also.

                        Yours sincerely,

                        Christopher Hendy.

Document 3

From - Major-General N. H. SPELLER
Director of Ordnance Services

Tel: 01-242-1688
Ext. 1393

First Avenue House,
High Holborn,
LONDON, W.C.1. V6HE

A/BR/68/41/Ord 3 (DOS)

SSgt J Brooks RAOC
c/o 16 Battalion
Royal Army Ordnance Corps
St George's Barracks
BICESTER
Oxon   *29* May 1974

Dear Brooks,

I have just heard of your praiseworthy
achievement in completing 289.64 miles, to
beat the existing British, Commonwealth and
European Walk Record at Aintree recently.

I know you must feel a little disappointed
at failing to break the World Record by so
narrow a margin. Nevertheless, your effort
on this occasion reflects credit on yourself,
the Corps and the Army as a whole.

Well done!

Yours sincerely,

N.H.Speller

Document 3a

Document 4

JOHN E BROOKS RAOC

British European and Commonwealth record holder for endurance walking plans to attempt the world record of 304 miles on the 1·65 mile motor racing circuit.
So far he has covered 289·64 miles on the same track, and 29 days later set out again on another charity walk from Birkenhead to Plymouth but was forced to retire after 291·75 miles because of bad weather.
But he soon recovered and was on the road again to raise £ 1200 plus, after walking for 24 hours around a 400 metre circuit. A distance of 109 miles was completed.
This event is a charitable one and all proceeds will go to the National Society for the Prevention of Cruelty to Children. (NSPCC)

PERSONAL

I suppose most of the readers of this programme wonder why I attempt to cover such distances. The answer is quite simple. To raise money to help those less fortunate than myself. For one moment stop and think of all the children in the world who are not able to walk or run around, through no fault of their own. Another aspect is the self satisfaction which one gets from walking, and I am convinced we are not all as mad as so many people seem to think!! Recently I participated in club events where as many as 150 individuals took part. It would be unfair to say that any type of long distance walking is easy for it is not. Like any other sport one must face the physical and mental hardships which so often occurs. But its the determination to succeed which helps to keep you going.

15 AUG 75.

Document 4a

Document 5

Document 6

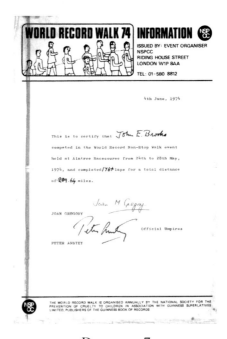

Document 7

Tricia Campbell

From:	Literature (Gordon McRae) [Literature@karcher.co.uk]
Sent:	23 November 2005 16:32
To:	Tricia Campbell
Subject:	Children- in- need

Dear Tricia

What a gem your Town Mayor John is!! I would vote him in every time.

Could you thank him from everyone here at Karcher, what a great job he has done. Everyone I have spoke to were very impressed by his professionalism and his ability to get on with everyone. I hope he enjoyed his tour round Karcher.Jenny sends her regards and her thanks for all your help on the day. The total we raised was £2868.00. there may be more to go into this as Karcher round up the figure.

John, if we could bottle you I would be your agent!!.Thanks for all your support,please keep up the good work.

Kind Regards
Gordon
Marketing

Document 8

Hearing Dogs
for Deaf People

Cllr John Brooks BEM - Mayor of Banbury
Banbury Town Council
The Town Hall
5B Bridge Street
Banbury
Oxfordshire
OX16 5QB

BANBURY TOWN COUNCIL

RECEIVED

Hearing Dogs for Deaf People
The Grange, Wycombe Road
Saunderton
Princes Risborough
Bucks HP27 9NS

T 01844 348 100
(voice and minicom)
F 01844 348 101
E info@hearing-dogs.co.uk
www.hearing-dogs.co.uk

11th May 2006

Dear Cllr Brooks,

On behalf of Hearing Dogs for Deaf People I would like to thank you for your very generous donation of £200.00 from your Mayoral year.

Hearing Dogs is celebrating its Silver Anniversary in 2007, and I am delighted to say that we have now trained over 1,200 dogs - with 750 active partnerships across the UK, and 22 in the Oxfordshire area. As Hearing Dogs receives no government funding we are totally reliant on the generosity of supporters to allow us to continue with our work.

I was unsure whether you had had an opportunity to visit Hearing Dogs, and therefore I would like to invite you to join us on one of our Thursday afternoon tours. These provide an excellent opportunity to learn more about our work and to see a Hearing Dog in action. If you would like to book a place on one of these please contact Reception on 01844 348100.

If you have any queries or require additional information on the work of Hearing Dogs, please do not hesitate to contact me on 01844 348136 or at Ruth.Dunkin@hearing-dogs.co.uk

Thank you again for your support.

Best Regards

Yours sincerely,

Ruth Dunkin
Ruth Dunkin
Regional Fundraiser
Hearing Dogs for Deaf People

Document 9

62-63 High Street, Banbury, OX16 5JJ

Tel: 01295 256111   e-mail: banburycake@nqo.com
Fax: 01295 268544   www.thisisoxfordshire.co.uk

John Brooks,
1 Homestead Road,
Bodicote Chase,
Banbury.   15 June 2006

Dear John,

I have been meaning to write this letter since the presentation night in the town hall at which
you distributed your charity cheques.

I want to express my thanks to yourself and Audrey for your co-operation and help during
your time as mayor of Banbury, and to congratulate you on such a successful year in office.

I also want to thank you for the pewter tankard which you presented to me that night.

It is something I will keep and treasure, and years to come when I am no longer involved with
local newspapers it will bring back very pleasant memories.

With the very best regards,

Julian

Document 10

Councillor John Brooks
Town Mayor
Banbury Town Council
The Town Hall
Bridge Street
Banbury
Oxfordshire OX16 5QB

19 May 2006

Dear Councillor Brooks

On behalf of Brainwave, I would like to thank you for making the very generous donation of
£100.00 from your Town Mayor's Fundraising Account, towards the rehabilitation costs
Leah from Banbury.

As you may know, Brainwave is reliant on voluntary contributions to maintain the Centre
and cover all it's overheads. We believe that the provision which Brainwave offers to
children and their parents is unique and we are committed to increasing the number of
children following our programmes of rehabilitation and development in the months ahead.
Your donation is a very important part of that provision and we are most grateful to you.

I will of course keep you informed of Leah's progress following her next reassessment.

Thank you once again for this very kind donation.

Yours sincerely

Margaret Preece (Mrs)
Direct Marketing Officer

 Huntworth Gate, Bridgwater, Somerset, TA6 6LQ
Telephone: (01278) 429089   Fax: (01278) 429622
E-mail: enquiries@brainwave.org.uk   www.brainwave.org.uk

Document 11

Document 12

Document 13

Fine Lady Bakeries Limited
Southam Road · Banbury · Oxon OX16 2RE
Tel: (01295) 227600 · Fax: (01295) 271430 · Email: info@flbltd.co.uk

SC/SH

9 February 2006

Councillor J Brooks
Town Mayor
1 Homestead Road
Bodicote Chase
BANBURY
Oxfordshire   OX16 9TW

Dear John

I thought I should write to say how much we enjoyed the Caribbean evening laid on by you as Banbury Town Mayor. It was a pleasure to be associated with the event and we were pleased to hear that the evening raised a good sum of money for your various charities.

I must just add a note of appreciation for the hard work that Tricia Campbell put into the evening, and indeed to the other events I have attended during your year.

Tricia always has a smiling face, which gives warmth to the occasions organised. I am sure a great deal of hard work, coupled with long and often unsocial hours are also required from her to give you the support and professionalism necessary to perform your Mayoral duties.

Please pass on my good wishes to her.

Yours sincerely

Steve Cook
Production Director

Registered Office: Roghorn, Mills, Northampton NN7 3JD. Registration No. 414692 England

Document 14

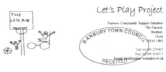

Let's Play Project

Fairway Community Support Initiative
The Fairway
Banbury
Oxon
OX16 0RS

Tel: 01295 275807
Fax: 01295 265073
Email: letsplay@wanadoo.co.uk

RECEIVED
BANBURY TOWN COUNCIL

Dear Mr Brooks,

I am writing to acknowledge the generous donation of £200 for the Let's Play Project. We were very pleased to receive it and will use it to help fund our summer activities.

We would also like to express our appreciation again for the interest you have shown in the project's work and, in particular, the time you gave during our charity launch in February.

With all good wishes,

Sarah Wallis, Manager

LOTTERY FUNDED

Document 15

Document 15b

BUCKINGHAM PALACE

At The Queen's command, I have been asked to thank you for your kind message of good wishes sent on the occasion of Her Majesty's eightieth Birthday. Your thoughtfulness in writing on this special Day was much appreciated and The Queen sends you her warm best wishes in return.

Special Assistant to the Private Secretary

June 2006

Document 16

Document 17

Document 18

LEONARD CHESHIRE

Central

The Oxfordshire Cheshire Home
Greenhill House
Adderbury
Banbury, Oxon OX17 3JB
Tel: 01295 810679
Fax: 01295 812711

Cllr John E Brooks
Town Mayor
The Town Hall
Bridge Street
Banbury
Ox16 5BQ

BANBURY TOWN COUNCIL
RECEIVED

22nd May 2006

Dear Sir

We write to thank you for the donation of £200.00 which represents the proceeds from your town mayors fundraising account

We are very appreciative of the support given to us, and are so very grateful for your kind donation.

Very best regards

PP Laura Giles

Sue Northcott
Service Manager

Creating opportunities with disabled people

Document 19

BANBURY TOWN COUNCIL

BANBURY ADVANCED MOTORISTS

Affiliated to
The Institute of Advanced Motorists

Tel No - 01869 241106

'The Willow'
Banbury Road
Bicester, Oxon
OX26 3NP

Councillor John Brooks BEM
The Mayor's Office,
The Town Hall,
Bridge Street,
Banbury,
Oxfordshire,
OX16 5QB

22nd May 2006

Dear John,
     On behalf of Banbury Advanced Motorists, I should like to thank you very much for including us in your Mayor's Charity this year. It was a great pleasure for my colleagues and I to attend the reception last week at which we received your gift.

     We had our regular Committee Meeting last Friday at which the gift was reported and my personal pleasure was echoed by the whole Committee; you can be assured that the £150 will be put to good use!

     Might I also take this opportunity to write that we are very pleased that you are currently one of our Associates? Now that your busy period is over(?) I trust that you can proceed speedily through the remainder of your Check Drives with Kromer Rogers to Test Standard, take the Final Check Drive, probably with our Chief Observer Chris Milner and take and pass your Advanced Test. With your permission we would make use of your progress as part of our publicity during the Summer to encourage more drivers in our area to raise their standards on the road. Perhaps some of your Councillor colleagues could be persuaded to follow your example?

     Once again thank you for the gift and my best wishes for the future.

     Yours sincerely,

Bernard Moore, Chairman

Document 20

BANBURY CIVIC SOCIETY
c/o 7 Spencer Court . Britannia Road . Banbury . Oxon . OX16 5EY : Tel. (01 295) 262 909

Cllr J E Brooks
1 Homestead Road
BANBURY
OX16 9TW

24 June 2006

Dear Cllr Brooks

The members of the Management Committee had hoped to welcome you to its first meeting of
the year, 2006-07, and were sorry that you were prevented from attending on 12th June .

One of the additional matters of business raised at that meeting was the state of the Thursday and
Saturday markets held in the town centre . Considerable concern was expressed at the meeting
over the apparent decline in standards, both in take-up and the range of outlets; there also seem
to be increasingly fewer stalls taken .

As the Committee does not have much knowledge of how the markets are organised, and by
whom, we had hoped to discover something of this from you, if you can indeed help us with your
personal knowledge of the situation .

We were therefore hoping that you could give us some help about this if you are able to be at the
next meeting of the Committee, on Monday, 10th July (all meetings being on the second Monday
of the month, with the exception of August).

Please let us know if this is possible . If you need to contact me before 30th June (when I return)
would you please instead get in touch with the Chairman, John Bell, whose telephone number is
Banbury 710005 .

With thanks, and my regards:

George Fryer, Hon. Secretary

Document 21

Girlguiding
Cherwell Division

Councillor John Brooks
The Town Hall
Bridge Street
Banbury
OX16 5QB

Laurel Cottage
Church Street
Barford St. Michael
Banbury
Oxon OX15 0UA

T: 01869 338017
e: susan.addison@virgin.net

26th May 2006

Dear Councillor Brooks,

I would like to thank you very much for the cheque for £150.00 you so kindly gave
to Girlguiding Cherwell at the Presentation Evening on 15th May. We were
absolutely delighted to be among the recipients of a cheque from your fund.

I do hope you have some splendid memories of your Mayoral year. It was a great
pleasure to meet and talk with you on a number of occasions during your time in
office.

Thank you again,

With best wishes

Susan M Addison
Division Commissioner, Girlguiding Cherwell

BANBURY TOWN COUNCIL
RECEIVED

Document 22

Document 23

Document 24

Our ref: CH/AM

18 May 2006

Ms Tricia Campbell,
Secretary to the Town Mayor,
Banbury Town Council
Town Council Offices
58 Bridge Street
Banbury
Oxfordshire OX16 3QB

30 Guthrie Street
Dundee DD1 5BS

Tel: (01382) 204446
Fax: (01382) 206771
E-mail: bbs@brittlebone.org

Dear Ms Campbell,

Family Conference & AGM
April 2006.

I refer to our letter of 1st December 2005 when you generously enclosed a donation of £100 to enable a family from Banbury to attend our Family Conference. Unfortunately no one from Banbury was able to travel to our Family Conference this year.

Would it be possible for us to keep this money on the understanding that we will only use it next year to help a family from Banbury to attend our Family Conference in 2007?

I look forward to hearing from you.

Yours sincerely,

Christine Hope
Christine Hope
Fundraising Officer

Freephone Helpline: 08000 28 24 59
Visit our Website at: www.brittlebone.org
Registered Charity No. England & Wales: 272100 Scotland: SCO 10901

Document 25

Banbury Town Council

Declaration of Acceptance of Office

I, John Elliot Brooks having been elected to the office of Town Mayor of Banbury Town Council, declare that I take that office upon myself, and will duly and faithfully fulfil the duties of it according to the best of my judgement and ability.

I undertake to observe the Code as to the conduct which is expected of Members of Banbury Town Council.

Signed

Date ....17 - 05 - 05...........

This declaration was made and signed before me.

Signed ....mDanby........

Proper Officer of the Council

* insert Member, Co-opted Member or Town Mayor

P\Council\Forms & Declarations\BTC New DECLARATION OF ACCEPTANCE OF OFFICE.doc

Document 26

Banbury Town Council

Mary Danby BA (Hons)
Town Clerk

Cllr John E Brooks BEM
Town Mayor

The Town Hall
Bridge Street
Banbury
Oxfordshire
OX16 5QB
Tel: 01295 250340
Fax: 01295 250820
E-mail: tricia.campbell@banbury.gov.uk
Please ask for: Tricia Campbell

Important Dates for your 2006 Diary

Fri 20th Jan.	Caribbean Evening (please see separate invitation)	Town Hall	7.30pm
Fri 24th Feb.	Volunteers reception	Town Hall	6.30pm
Fri 24th March	Tea Dance	Town Hall	2.00pm
Sun 9th April	ATC 65th Anniversary	Town Hall	
Fri 28th April	Dinner & Dance	College	7.30pm
Mon. 15th May	Chq presentation evening	Town Hall	7.00pm
Tues 16th May	Annual Meeting	Town Hall	6.30pm
Sun 2nd July	Civic Sunday & Hobby Horse Festival	People's Park	2.00pm
Sat 2nd Sept.	Organ Festival & Town Criers National Competition	Banbury Town	all day
Sun 17th Sept.	Battle of Britain	St. Mary's Church	11am
Sun 1st Oct.	Banbury Canal Day	Canalside	all day
Sat 11th Nov	Charities Bazaar	Town Hall	all day
Sun 12th Nov	Remembrance Day	St. Mary's Church	10am
Fri 1st Dec	Toy Appeal	Town Hall	5.00pm

Document 26a

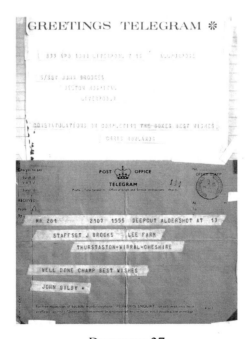

Document 27

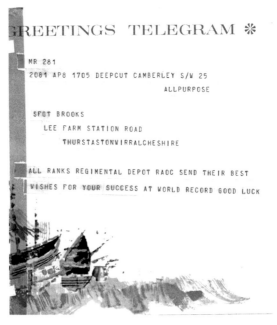

GREETINGS TELEGRAM ❈

MR 281

2081 AP8 1705 DEEPCUT CAMBERLEY S/W 25

ALLPURPOSE

SFGT BROOKS

LEE FARM STATION ROAD

THURSTASTONWIRRALCHESHIRE

ALL RANKS REGIMENTAL DEPOT RAOC SEND THEIR BEST

WISHES FOR YOUR SUCCESS AT WORLD RECORD GOOD LUCK

Document 27a

From: Brigadier P J O'B Minogue

Headquarters
Central Ordnance Depot
Bicester
Oxfordshire
OX6 0LD

Bicester 3311 Ext. 500

BIC/COMD/5

Staff Sergeant J Brooks RAOC
16 Bn RAOC
St George's Barracks
Arncott
Bicester, Oxon   30th May 1974

My Dear Stuff,

I feel sure that many of us from COD Bicester, as I was,
were closely following your progress on the radio bulletins
during last weekend. To complete 290 miles was indeed a
splendid achievement and I know how disappointed you must
be at failing to break the world record by such a
comparatively small distance. However the European and
Commonwealth records are now in your pocket and, with your
determination, the world record really doesn't stand a
chance.

It is your kind of effort which gives such a very good name
to our Corps and to the Army. We are all very proud of you.

Yours very sincerely

Document 28

162

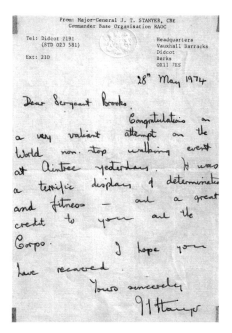

From: Major-General J. T. STANYER, CBE
Commander Base Organisation RAOC

Tel: Didcot 2191
(STD 023 581)

Ext: 210

Headquarters
Vauxhall Barracks
Didcot
Berks
OX11 7ES

28ᵗʰ May 1974

Dear Sergeant Brooks,

Congratulations on a very valiant attempt on the World non-stop walking event at Aintree yesterday. It was a terrific display of determination and fitness — and a great credit to you and the Corps. I hope you have recovered.

Yours sincerely

J T Stanyer

Document 28a

Document 29

The
Katharine
House
Hospice

Councillor John E Brooks
The Town Hall
Bridge Street
Banbury
Oxon OX16 5QB

East End, Adderbury
Banbury, OX17 3NL
Tel. 01295 811866
Fax: 01295 810993
Fundraising & Lottery Office
Tel. 01295 812161
e-mail: general@khh.org.uk
www.khh.org.uk

23 May 2006

Dear Councillor Brooks

Thank you, on behalf of everyone at Katharine House, for your kind donation of £100.00 from the Town Mayor's Fundraising Account. This contribution is very much appreciated and will be invaluable in helping our medical and nursing teams continue to provide care and comfort for our patients and their families here in Adderbury.

2006 sees the fifteenth anniversary of the opening of the hospice. Maintenance of the facilities here is an ongoing task and we have recently completed work on the exterior of the building and grounds. This year, for the first time since opening, we will have to refurbish the inpatient unit. This will involve replacing carpets, curtains, linen and furniture and also re-upholstering some of the larger sofas and chairs. This will be our major maintenance project for the year, with an estimated cost in excess of £50,000.

Please find enclosed your receipt along with our grateful thanks to the Town Council for its continued and valued support.

Kind regards

Yours sincerely

Sheila Norton (Mrs)
Fundraising Administrator

Thank you very much for your support of the Katharine House Hospice. Your name will be added to our database as a valued supporter but if you would prefer not to receive information on Hospice activities then please tick this box □ and return to Katharine House Hospice, FREEPOST, East End, Adderbury, Banbury, Oxon OX17 3BR. If you have already informed us that you do not wish to be on our database then there is no need to take any action.

President
The Hon. Peter Ward

Patrons
The Duke of Marlborough
Lord Saye and Sele

Katharine House Hospice provides specialist palliative care in pleasant surroundings.

Registered Charity No. 297099 Limited Company No. 2102091

Document 30

28. CROMWELL ROAD,
BANBURY,
OXON.
26-11-2005.
TELEPHONE:-01295 267238.

DEAR MAYOR,

THANK YOU VERY MUCH FOR COMING TO HELP RAISE MONEY ON FRIDAY NIGHT (25-11-2005). AT OUR PRIZE BINGO, AT HARDWICK COMMUNITY HALL.

IT WAS LOVELY TO MEET YOU IN PERSON. I HOPE YOU ENJOYED YOURSELF. IF MYSELF OR MY MUM AND DAD CAN HELP YOU IN ANY-WAY PLEASE DO NOT HESITATE TO RING ME.

I GO TO STEPPING STONES MYSELF AS I HAVE GOT DISABILITIES AND VERY BAD LEARNING PROBLEMS AND CLASSED AS DISABLED.

I LOOK FORWARD TO MEETING YOU AGAIN IN THE NEAR FUTURE.

ONCE AGAIN THANK YOU VERY MUCH FOR PUTTING YOURSELF OUT, AND COMING TO SUPPORT MY MUM AND DADS EFFORTS TO RAISE MONEY FOR STEPPING STONES.

YOURS,

RACHEL SMITH.

Document 31

BANBURY AND DISTRICT TWINNING ASSOCIATION

Chairman:
Ron Barnett
39 Waterloo Drive
Banbury
OX16 3QN
01295 278810
Ron.Barnett@BTInternet.com

Treasurer:
Gareth Jeremy
18 Burlington Gardens
Banbury
OX16 9NQ
01295 266404

24 May 2006

Dear Councillor John Brooks

Banbury and District Twinning Association

I write on behalf of the Association to thank you for all the support that you have given us during the past year.

I would also like to thank you for the extremely generous donation to the Association made from your Charity Fund. This will go a long way to help us continue to foster friendship and understanding between the people of Banbury and our Twin Towns.

On a personal basis, it has been a great pleasure to work with you, and I hope that we will continue to do so in furtherance of the Twinning Association's aims.

Again, my very grateful thanks for everything that you have done to support the Association during your term of office as Town Mayor and our President.

Yours sincerely

Ron Barnett
Chairman

Councillor John Brooks
Banbury Town Council
The Town Hall
Bridge Street
Banbury
OX16 5QB

Document 32

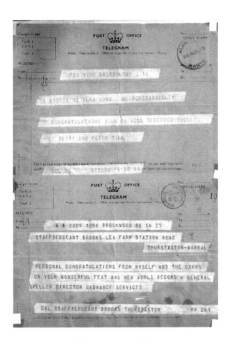

Document 33

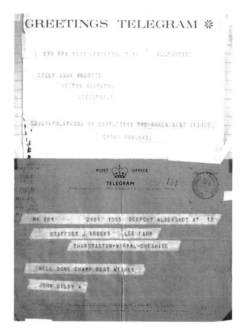

Document 33a

Document 34

BUCKINGHAM PALACE

Warrant Officer Class 2 J. Brooks, RAOC,
Liverpool Society for the Prevention
of Cruelty to Children.

Please convey the sincere thanks
of The Queen to all members of the Liverpool
Branch of the National Society for the
Prevention of Cruelty to Children for
their kind message of loyal greetings, sent
on the occasion of their Centenary. As
Patron of the Society, Her Majesty received
this message with much pleasure, and
sends her best wishes for the success of
their celebrations and activities and for
a happy and successful Centenary Year.

PRIVATE SECRETARY.

3rd June, 1983.

Document 35

BUCKINGHAM PALACE

19th May, 1983.

Dear M. Martin.

Thank you for your letter of
4th May with which you enclosed a message
to The Queen from the National Society for
the Prevention of Cruelty to Children

This has been laid before Her
Majesty, who has commanded me to send you
the attached reply.

Yours sincerely

Robert Fellowes.

Warrant Officer Class 1 F. Morton, RAOC.

Document 35a

167